Facing the Crises of Life

by
Rabbi Joshua O. Haberman

New Publishing Partners
Washington, DC

Published by New Publishing Partners
2510 Virginia Avenue
Suite 702N
Washington, DC 20037
www.npp-publishing.com

ISBN-13: 978-0-9882500-1-7
ISBN-10: 0988250012

Cover design, book design, and editing by Deborah Lange

Cover painting by Debi Sacks

Printed in Canada

Other books by Joshua O. Haberman:

*Philosopher of Revelation: The Life and Thought of
S. L. Steinheim*

*The God I Believe In: Conversations about Judaism with
14 Leading Rabbis, Philosophers, and Novelists*

*Healing Psalms: The Dialogues with God that Help You
Cope with Life*

*Three Cities in the Making of a Rabbi: Vienna, Washington
and Jerusalem: A Memoir*

To my beloved Maxine in celebration of
our 70th wedding anniversary

Acknowledgments

I am deeply grateful to Audrey Adler Wolf for helpful suggestions and to Deborah D. Lange for meticulous editing of my book. Thank you also to Paul H. Levine for reviewing the final manuscript.

Contents

Preface

Deeper than any bond which unites people, such as the same language, nationality, or religion, is the common experience of certain life crises. Sooner or later, everyone suffers illness, rejection, conflict with a spouse or life partner, the decline of aging, doubt about life's meaning, and the fear of death. Nobody escapes these crises but knowing what to expect may help us prepare and better cope with these crises.

1 Illness

The Bible's first event in the history of mankind is the expulsion from Paradise. With grim realism we are told that life on earth is not a bowl of cherries. It is full of pain and hard labor:

> By the sweat of your brow shall you eat bread....for dust you are and to dust you shall return. (Gen. 3,19)

It is a dire assessment, surpassed only by Thomas Hobbes's summation of life as "solitary, poor, nasty, brutish, and short."

We all share the gut feeling that life is precarious. We are haunted by an undercurrent of insecurity. At any point in life we may suffer injury or illness. Sooner or later, we succumb to one of these ailments.

How does a health crisis affect our outlook on life and how can we cope with it?

The immediate impact of illness on the patient is a shrinkage of interest. The fears that come with illness crowd out other concerns. Illness tends to make us self-centered. The world is reduced to the dimensions of our sick-room. There is truth in William Hazlitt's statement that "the least pain in our little finger gives us more concern and uneasiness than the destruction of millions of our fellow beings."

There are exceptions. John Gunther's brilliant teen-age son Johnny suffered from a brain tumor. He needed two operations within 14 months. Just two weeks before his death at 18, he passed his Columbia University entrance examination. After his first operation, the doctors advised the parents that Johnny should be told the truth of his condition. The parents asked the doctors to do it. The surgeon then went to see Johnny alone and disclosed to him the full gravity of a brain tumor. The boy listened carefully, looked the doctor in the eye, and asked, "How shall we break it to my parents?"

Aside from understandable self-centeredness due to suffering, patients grow overly sensitive about real or imagined neglect. The sick person tends to feel like an outcast, isolated and shunned. One of the psalmists moans, "My friends and companions, even relatives, stay away." (Ps. 38.12) Another complains, "I am forgotten as a dead man out of mind." (Ps. 31.13)

In my visits with patients I have often sensed the unspoken question of the sufferer: "Why is this happening to me? Where have I gone wrong?" Such questions soon expand into a re-assessment of one's life. How important is my work? Where else shall I put time, energies, and means? What changes shall I make? In my work? My daily routines? My life in the family?

Many resolutions are made on one's sickbed; regrettably, not all outlast the illness. One late night, a member of my congregation called me from the Cleveland Clinic. "Rabbi," he said with trembling voice," I am going in for open heart surgery. Please, pray for me. If I come out alive, I shall be in temple every week." He came out all right but not to temple.

Illness should not be abhorred as absolute evil. With its hurt and harm go some benefits. Robert Burton in his *The Anatomy of Melancholy* wrote: "Sickness is the mother of modesty, as it puts us in mind of our mortality, and...pulls us by the ear and makes us know ourselves."

One discovery we owe to illness is that the world goes on without us. No one is indispensable, not in one's profession, job, business, or community. Illness knocks us off the pedestal of pride. It cuts us down to size. The patient is likely to revise his self-image to more modest and realistic proportions. Good health and strength can give us a macho illusion. Psalm 30 puts it well: "As long as I felt secure, I said, I shall never be moved; I was a fortress on a mountain." (Ps. 30.7-8)

Thomas Mann's monumental novel, *The Magic Mountain,* shows how the hero, Hans Castorp, grows intellectually and matures during his prolonged illness in a Swiss sanatorium. It illustrates Thoreau's assertion: "It is healthy to be sick sometimes."

How can we best cope with illness and abnormal anxiety over our health, which is but a step away from depression?

There is no better antidote to illness than hopefulness. Scientists explain it as a sensory/neurological give and take between mind and body. The messages sent from body to brain and back again deeply influence our capacity for cure. A change of mind can change our neurochemistry. Belief and expectation can block pain by releasing the brain's endorphins and enkephalins, matching the effect of morphine. Hope offsets fear with favorable effects on respiration and circulation.

But how can you be hopeful when racked by pain, in serious illness with a poor prognosis? You may draw hope from previous experiences of recovery. The agnostic G.B. Shaw would not credit God for it but he acknowledged recovery as one of life's great joys: "I enjoy convalescence. It is the part that makes illness worthwhile."

If you believe that God is involved in every life, you will recognize God's doing in the power of healing. Miraculously, diseased organs and tissues repair themselves. "I am fearfully and wonderfully made," exclaimed the psalmist. (Ps. 139.14)

The God who allows illness to afflict us also endows us with healing power. As is said in the Book of Job:

He makes sore, and binds up again,
The hand that wounds is the hand that makes us whole again.
(Job 5.18)

Hopefulness has a twin, which is crucial to recovery, and that is will power. The Book of Proverbs says, "The spirit of a man will sustain him in his infirmity." (Pr. 18.14) I like to refer to a case in my family. Alvin, a cousin of my wife, Maxine, lived in Buffalo. In his early twenties Alvin was disabled by ulcerative colitis, then considered incurable. He was hardly able to hold down food and his body turned to skin and bones. Alvin became an invalid, a shut-in, under doctor's orders not to step out of his room. Unable to finish his education, his future looked grim. He was a home-bound prisoner under a life sentence.

Years passed. We lost touch. However, on a trip to Buffalo we had an opportunity to see Alvin again. When we visited him in his apartment, we saw no change in his appearance, but there was a smile on his face. "I am doing well," he said.

"And what are you doing?"

The answer was hard to believe: "I am in the ship-rigging business." Sensing our astonishment, he explained how he managed to do it all by telephone. After reading everything there was to know about all kinds of ships, from sailboats to steamers, memorizing lists of nautical equipment and their suppliers, he would contact by phone the captains of incoming ships at Buffalo's lakeside. Relying on the phenomenal memory of details he had developed, he visualized whatever equipment the captains were talking about and took orders, even though he had never seen the equipment. In time he built up a prosperous business.

Alvin's case illustrates some of the compensatory abilities often gained by people stricken with an incurable illness or a handicap. It is as though God takes away with one hand, and gives back with the other.

A PRAYER

Almighty God, Creator of all there is, giver of life. I am Your creature, a mere speck of dust in the universe, and yet, even as I think of You, I know that You must also be mindful of me. Every moment I depend on You and Your power to keep me alive. I turn to You in great need. I am weak and ill. I need Your help.

Guide the physicians and nurses in their care of me. Grant them a portion of Your spirit and let their kindness reflect Your love.

I entrust My spirit into Your care, in sleep and upon awakening; and with my spirit, my body too. You are with me. I shall not fear. Amen.

2 Failure

William James, philosopher and psychologist, in a letter to H. G. Wells a century ago, expressed disgust at the American worship of the "bitch-goddess success," which, he added, is usually given "a squalid cash interpretation." In this respect, nothing has changed. We emphasize, we glorify, and we glamorize success in every area of human activity. We instill in our children ambition and striving for success. Yet the reality is that along with occasional success, everyone suffers failures: in work, in rearing families, or in personal relations.

The Anglican cleric Bernard Iddings Bell defined a good education as "not so much one which prepares a man to succeed in the world as one which enables him to sustain failure."

Inability to sustain failure is the stuff tragedy is made of. It provides the plot for Arthur Miller's play *Death of a Salesman.* Willy Loman, first demoted from his company and then fired, despairs at his failure. Dreading inability to support the family and pay off the mortgage, Willy Loman commits suicide. He lacked what Riesman called the "nerve of failure;" that is, the ability to sustain failure and go on with life.

No human being can live long without miscalculating, making mistakes, suffering losses, or stumbling into a detour that derails his life and should have been marked "Wrong Way."

What if you are unsuccessful?

The answer is: change course, move in another direction, try something else.

Eddie Cantor began his career as an office boy with a financial firm on Wall Street and was fired. He changed course, tried other ways of making a living, and discovered his real talent as a comedian. Being fired from that Wall Street office was a defeat which turned into the springboard to immense success.

We must not let failure paralyze us in hopelessness. Some of the world's greatest achievers passed through humiliating failure. Napoleon Bonaparte was one of the worst students in military school. He graduated number 42 in a class of 43. England's most brilliant philosopher, David Hume, was described by his mother in his boyhood as "uncommonly weak-minded." Isaac Newton, the most brilliant scientist in history, was still so backward in his upper teens that he had to be taken out of school.

The first rule in coping with failure is to hope to do better another day or in another way.

Celebrity careers illustrate the point: Jay Leno applied for a job at Woolworth's but failed the employment test, only to become one of our most popular entertainers.

Barbara Walters was told in 1957 by the Executive Producer of *60 Minutes* to stay out of television. But that turn-down did not keep her from reaching the top and being elected to the Television Hall of Fame.

A boy from Texas was kicked out of Southwest Texas State Teachers College and drove to California in a 1918 Model T Ford with four friends; there he worked as an elevator operator, a grape picker, a dishwasher, a law clerk, and an auto mechanic. Returning to Texas, he tried politics, and so Lyndon Johnson became President of the United States.

The responses to failure that I have illustrated so far with various examples may be summed up in a single word: perseverance. Ability is not enough to achieve.

> Talent made a poor Appearance
> Until he married Perseverance.
> (Arthur Guiterman)

Perseverance also has the Biblical stamp of approval. It is one of the virtues of the righteous; he does not quit. As the Bible puts it, "The righteous falls seven times and rises up again." (Pr. 24.16)

There is another way of coping with failure, possibly a more profound and helpful way, and that is re-assessing the criteria by which you judge success and failure. Henry David Thoreau was considered by many of his contemporaries a loser because instead of seeking riches, he chose to reduce his material needs to the barest minimum. He preferred walks through the woods to working long hours in an office. He explained his departure from the norm: "If a man does not keep pace with his companions, perhaps it is because he hears a different drummer." He chose to live by a set of values different from those by which others measure success.

Edwin Arlington Robinson wrote a poem which likewise rejects the popular criteria by which success and failure are judged:

When Richard Corey went downtown
We people on the pavement looked at him;
He was a gentleman from sole to crown,
Clean favored, and imperially slim.

And he was rich, yes, richer than a king
And admirably schooled in every grace.
In fine, we thought that he was everything
To make us wish that we were in his place.

So on we worked, and waited for the light,
And went without meat, and cursed the bread;
And Richard Corey, one calm summer night,
Went home and put a bullet through his head.
(*Richard Corey*)

If what counts are the things that money can't buy—serenity, contentment, and a loving family—then very few of the rich and famous make it, whatever their so-called "success" might be. Contrast the life style of the Richard Coreys in this world with the picture drawn by Psalm 128:

When you eat the labor of your hands,
Happy shall you be, and it shall be well with you.
Your wife shall be as a fruitful vine, inside your house;
Your children like olive plants round about your table.
Behold, so shall the man be blessed who reveres God.

According to these lines, you are a success if you are self-supporting and draw happiness from your family circle; not necessarily rich, but beloved by spouse and children, with a roof over your head and food on the table.

I would go further and say: if you make a go of your marriage but fail in everything else, you are a success. A license plate I once saw suggests a way of strengthening your marriage. It said simply: YES DEAR.

When Margaret Thatcher and her husband, Dennis, moved to #10 Downing St., a reporter asked Dennis, "Who wears the pants in your house?" He answered, "I do, and I also wash and iron them."

What if, in your own eyes, you have failed in your family life as spouse or parent and have failed in your work or career? The answer is: acknowledge your mistakes and turn your life around. If you think that you're at the end of your rope, listen to the psalmist who said, "Cast your burden upon God and He will sustain you." (Ps. 55.23). You are not the only player in your life. Help can come to you in ways you can't even imagine. Don't quit.

The story is told of a woman who took her little boy to a piano concert by the great Paderewski at Carnegie Hall. Her six-year old son had shown an ear for music. The mother thought that a concert by the great master would make the boy more diligent in his piano lessons. She chatted with the lady on her left until the lights were dimmed. She turned to the seat on her right. It was empty. The boy had disappeared. In distress she looked for the nearest usher, but the curtain rose and, to her horror, she spotted the little boy on the stage, at the grand piano, banging out *Jingle Bells*! At this point Paderewski entered, bent down to the little boy, whispered, "keep playing," and reached over to accompany the boy with a grand flourish of music of symphonic splendor. The audience was thrilled and broke into thunderous applause. Many who witnessed the spectacle in time forgot what else Paderewski had played that night but long remembered the musical embellishment he had given to the little boy's childish performance. Similarly, there are times when our own fumbling efforts are raised to great achievement by the unexpected intervention of some helper, even God, as long as we don't quit.

3 Rejection

If human experiences were to be ranked according to the frequency of their occurrence, the experience of rejection would be close to the top. From childhood to old age, we are bound to be rebuffed many, many times. Rejection by one or both parents is not uncommon and most painful. The ill-favored child may never get over it.

Children are no less cruel to one another by rejecting an unpopular classmate and excluding the child from a circle of friends.

The universal experience of rejection has inspired many a novel, one of which made its author, Wolfgang Goethe, world famous at the age of 25. *The Sorrows of Werther* tells of a young man in love with Lotte, who decides to marry his friend Albert. Rejected, Werner commits suicide. Millions of readers shed copious tears and the story was discussed all over the world. Chinese paintings on glass illustrated the rejection of Werther. Napoleon is said to have read the novel nine times.

The eccentric sage of ancient Greece, Diogenes, was seen begging from a statue. Asked why he would do such a futile thing, he answered, "I am practicing being rejected."

Not all who suffer rejection are crushed by it. Many rise to great heights despite or because of it. I had a distinguished neighbor at my former home in Potomac, Admiral Arleigh Burke. Once, having a drink together at my place, I got him to talk about his life and career. "How did you, born and raised in land-locked Colorado, get into the Navy?"

Burke answered, "When I was about 17, not doing well in school and idling my time away, my father blew his top and yelled: 'Arleigh, you'll never amount to anything.'"

Feeling rejected, Arleigh ran away from home and joined the Navy. Determined to prove his father wrong, he rose through the ranks to the very top as chief of naval operations from 1955 to 1961. His was a spectacular career, triggered by a rejection that turned into a powerful incentive to make changes and prove his mettle in life.

Ernest Hemingway and Robert St. John were schoolmates in Chicago. One day, the English teacher returned papers to both with very low marks and the comment, "You have no talent for writing."

Rejection only fired the ambition of both to prove the teacher wrong. Hemingway won the Nobel prize in literature and Robert St. John became a leading journalist, war time reporter, and author of some 20 books.

Virtually all great achievers had to cope, at one time or the other, with under-estimation or rejection.

John Grisham, author of a string of best sellers, had his first novel rejected by 16 agents and a dozen publishing houses.

Sigmund Freud had to struggle many years for recognition. Academicians did not think much of psychoanalysis. They ignored or disparaged his work. His first ground-breaking book, *The Interpretation of Dreams,* yielded a mere $250 in royalties in the first eight years of publication.

Elvis Presley was told by his high school music teacher in Memphis that he couldn't sing.

Lucille Ball came to New York at age 15 to enroll in John Murray Anderson's drama school, where she was told repeatedly that she had no talent and should go home. Turned down by several Broadway theatres, she worked as a waitress and soda jerk in a drug store before becoming the star of one of TV's most successful comedy shows.

No one really knows your full potential. Rejection may well be the best thing that could happen to you if it challenges you to reassess your abilities and make changes which lead you to your goal. Success and failure are not in your circumstances but within you. No matter what others think of you, your own sense of worth is the key to your destiny, as Longfellow said so well:

Not in the clamor of the crowded street,
Not in the shouts and plaudits of the throng
But in ourselves, are triumph and defeat.
(*The Poets*)

The early Christian Church is one of history's most telling examples of the rise from rejection to triumph. For two centuries Christians in Rome were persecuted, tortured, thrown to the lions, and crucified by the thousands. Yet, steadfast in faith, they triumphed.

Christianity became the state religion of Rome. It largely shaped Western civilization and won the allegiance of one third of mankind.

When it comes to rejection, Jews are the champions of that experience. For some 20 centuries the Jewish people suffered persecution, expulsion, and degradation, yet they never saw themselves as inferior to their persecutors. In spite of or because of their historic ordeal, Jews developed exceptional intellectual and spiritual qualities. They are disproportionately represented among the foremost scientists, thinkers, and sages of the Western World and the Orient. Even after the Holocaust, the Jewish people continued to rise to high levels of achievement, an admired ethnic component among the nations.

Countless are the formerly downtrodden, despised, and rejected—Jews, Christians, people of all faiths and races—whose rise to greatness bears witness to the psalmist's line:

The stone which the builders rejected has become the chief cornerstone. (Ps. 118.22)

4 Marriage Problems

With the American divorce rate at about 50 percent, it may be said that for every more or less satisfied couple there is one that is mismatched, miserable, and heading for the divorce court. It would take more than a book to analyze all the components of a good marriage or the many possible reasons for a failed marriage. I would limit myself to only two prescriptions for maintaining a stable marriage.

To begin with, marriage partners should know what it is that makes for the strongest bond in their relationship. Some would say "mutual attraction" or speak mysteriously about their "chemistry." Also often mentioned are "common interests" and other factors that strengthen the marriage. All these are important, but what is most important is the degree of satisfaction each spouse gives to the needs of the other. The person who satisfies some of your needs is one you want to be with. The more of your needs are satisfied by that person, the greater will be your attachment.

Closely related to this is the second requirement for a solid marriage: the ability of the couple to resolve disputes.

It is only natural that two personalities will differ at times. If in the course of an argument, reasons do not persuade, the discussion will turn into a quarrel. How do you stop it before it becomes mutually abusive? Let's say a couple of limited means argue over what to buy, a new car or new furniture. He wants the car, she, the furniture. They can't afford both. Compromise is not feasible in this case. It has got to be one or the other. Who should yield?

If neither spouse is willing, they'll go on arguing, repeating the reasons already stated, only louder and angrier each time. Prolonged arguments are dangerous. Within hours of strife, the couple's tender feelings are replaced by resentment and mutual respect is lost. If this goes on for a few days, the marriage is headed for serious trouble. At this point, one or the other must recognize how much pain this is causing and give in.

Remember this: when compromise doesn't work, one or the other must make the sacrifice and yield in the interest of their marriage. It is a sacrifice out of love, and as long as love lasts, spouses will make those sacrifices for each other. If a quarrel temporarily overshadows love, the sacrifice that ends the quarrel will quickly renew and even intensify the couple's loving feelings for each other.

5 Worries

Worry casts its shadow over everything. It affects you physically, robs you of sleep, ruins your appetite, drives you to drink or take drugs, and makes you sick. What can you do about it?

We worry when threatened. The immediate reaction is fear. Our worries are fears in different disguises: Health worries are driven by fear of pain and disablement; money worries, by fear of poverty and dependency; work-related worries, by fear of humiliation and loss of status.

Most people worry about not getting things done. There are just too many problems to deal with. They get bewildered thinking about all the chores of the day. You can calm your nerves if you look at all these demands and duties as a bank teller does. No matter how large the crowd of people waiting to be served, the teller knows that people will come up in line just one at a time. So it is with your problems. They don't all have to be handled at once, but rather one at a time.

A number of psalms suggest ways of coping with worry. Psalm 56 says: "In God do I trust; I will not be afraid. What can man do unto me?" (Ps. 56.12)

The psalmist knew as well as you and I that others can do us harm. But trust in God can calm our fears. Trust in God means that God plays a role in our life; that God wants us to live and helps us overcome illness and evil.

Fears and worries make you obsessive; you can see nothing but the thing that threatens you. The way out is suggested in one of the most beloved psalms:

I will lift up mine eyes unto the mountains;
From whence shall my help come?
My help comes from God Who made heaven and earth.
God will not suffer your foot to be moved;
He that keeps Israel does neither slumber nor sleep.
God is your keeper;
God is your shade upon your right hand.
The sun shall not smite you by day,

Nor the moon by night.
God shall keep you from all evil;
He shall keep your soul.
God shall guard your going out and your coming in
From this time forth and for ever.
(Psalm 121)

This psalm projects life in a larger context. You may feel trapped and defeated because you are too narrowly focused on the problem at hand. When you can't see anything beyond the limits of the present situation, extend your horizon and look beyond this moment and beyond this place.

During the battle of Waterloo, a junior officer stormed into the command tent of the Duke of Wellington with the alarming news: "Napoleon's forces are upon us!"

Wellington, unfazed, said, "Young man, get yourself a bigger map and you'll see that we have Napoleon surrounded."

Realism, looking only at the facts of the moment, may be short-sighted. Faith projects a bigger map of life in which what seems like defeat today may turn out to be victory tomorrow. Do not become too narrowly focused on today's problems, however threatening these may seem. Help may come from sources you cannot see or even imagine. Countless are the possibilities of change.

When hard pressed by a multitude of tasks, you get that sinking feeling of falling behind and failing. Time is flying and you see no way of catching up. You are afraid of the consequences. That's the time when you start day-dreaming about ways of escape, as did the psalmist:

O that I had the wings of a bird!
I would fly away and find rest;
Surely, I would flee far off;
I would lodge in the wilderness;
I should soon find me a refuge.
(Ps. 55.7-9)

But escape, as the psalmist found out, was no solution. Neither is it for those who run away when harassed and overburdened. After trying various escape routes such as drinking, gambling, and other adventures, we must still face our problems. When you see no way out of your difficulties and problems, do as did the psalmist: humble yourself and ask for God's help:

> As for me, I call to God;
> God will deliver me.
> Evening, morning, and noon,
> I complain and moan, and God hears my voice...
> Cast your burden on God and He will sustain you.
> (Ps. 55.17-18, 23)

When your tasks and problems are too big to handle, let go and pray for God's help. Ask that God may sustain you. The point is not to do nothing, but to bide your time and have faith; to try again to tackle your problems another time. By calling on God to cast your burden upon Him, you are saying, "I am not the only player in my life." Tomorrow, other circumstances, other persons may come to your aid; you may discover new resources with which to manage your problems. God may open your eyes to see new ways. Help may come from unexpected places. "Cast your burden upon God" means "Don't carry the world on your shoulders; let go and let God."

One of the psalmists counsels us to "order our affairs," that is, to do whatever you can to prepare for what lies ahead. Then, be steadfast and trust God:

> Well it is with the man...that orders his affairs rightfully.
> He shall never be moved;
> He shall not be afraid of evil tidings;
> His heart is steadfast, trusting in God.
> His heart is established, he shall not be moved.
> (Ps 112.5-7)

A PRAYER

Dear God:

   I turn to You, Who is enthroned on the prayers of all who trust in You, because I need Your help. I am hard-pressed. I fear I cannot do what I should do. I am afraid I shall not succeed. I worry by day and am restless at night. I worry about meeting the expectations of my dear one, of co-workers and superiors.

   In my weakness, give me strength; in my distress, let me draw hope from Your presence; in my fear, show me the way out of my difficulties, the way I should go. You are the God of my salvation, my shield and protector. For You I wait. In You I trust. Amen.

6 Depression

The pursuit of happiness, according to our *Declaration of Independence*, is an "unalienable right" but its attainment is not guaranteed. Even when we enjoy happiness, it is sporadic, not a permanent condition. We swing back and forth between happy and unhappy moods. Mood changes are normal. Generally cheerful persons will also have their low-spirited days. But, if you sink into long periods of unrelieved gloom and you can't snap out of it, you suffer from melancholy or depression. A depression may be triggered by bereavement, ill health, material loss, failure, rejection, the breakup of a relationship, and various other setbacks. It is bad enough if you know the cause of your distress, but far worse if you can't tell why you are sad. Such is the case of the psalmist in Psalm 42: "My tears have been my food day and night...Why are you cast down, O my soul? Why do you sigh within me?" (Ps. 42.4, 6)

In his misery, the psalmist remembers happier days: "These things I remember, and pour out my soul within me: how I walked with the crowd and led them to the house of God, with joy and praise, a multitude celebrating the holiday." (Ps. 42.5)

But memories of happy days could make you feel worse about your present misery. In despair, the psalmist yearns for God: "As the deer pants after the water brooks, so pants my soul after You, O God. My soul thirsts for God, for the living God." (Ps. 42. 2-3)

In the very outreach to God, hope awakens in the psalmist. He reassures himself: "Hope in God! I shall yet praise Him for the salvation of His presence." (Ps. 42. 6, 12)

If you cannot shake off your dark mood, do as the psalmist. Voice your feelings and ask for God's help:

> Be gracious unto me, O God, for I languish away. Heal me, O God, for I am frightened. And You, O God, how much longer? Deliver me my sighing; every night tears flood my bed...Mine eye is dimmed because of grief. (Ps. 6.3-5, 7-8)

Having reached rock-.bottom, the psalmist experiences the answer to prayer:

God has listened to my weeping. God has heard my petition; God accepted my prayer. (Ps. 6.9-10)

One of the reasons for hope is the fact that nothing stays the same. Things change, even problems which now distress you. Psalm 113 tells of dramatic reversals in the lives of men and women. God, the psalmist believes, is involved in our lives. God "raises the poor out of the dust and lifts up the needy out of the dung, to set him with princes...[God enables] the barren woman to become a joyful mother of children in her house." (Ps. 113.7-9) The message is: Do not despair. Things can change very suddenly. If you believe in God's care, you'll trust that God will help you.

Legend tells that King Solomon had a ring engraved with the words "This too will pass." Whenever he was downcast, he would look at his ring and be cheered by the thought that the cause of his vexation would pass as does everything else.

The 30th psalm celebrates one of those happy reversals in life:

Weeping may tarry for the night, but joy comes in the morning...You turned my mourning into dancing; you removed my sackcloth and girded me with gladness so that I might sing praise to You and not be silent; O my God, I will give thanks unto You for ever. (Ps. 30.6, 12-13)

If your problem is a sense of failure, dissatisfaction with your career, and a general lack of contentment, try to make an inventory of your life. Count not only what is missing in your life, but also what you have gotten; not only where you have failed, but also what you have achieved; not only wherein you fall short, but also what you *can* do; not only the things that went wrong, but also what turned out right. Can you see, hear, talk, walk, and take care of yourself? Can you breathe, eat, and sleep? Does your heart beat without pain? Do you have a home? Family? Friends who care?

Acknowledge all that is good and give thanks for it. Thanksgiving and happiness are twins. If there is anything at all for which you should be grateful, say so and joy will chase away some of your gloom. Practice thanksgiving daily. Yon might repeat the words of the psalmist:

Blessed be the name of God from this time forth and for ever, from the rising of the sun unto the going down thereof, God's name is to be praised...Bless God and all that is within me bless His holy name. Bless God, O my soul, and forget not His benefits; Who forgives all your iniquity; Who heals all your diseases; Who redeems your life from the grave; Who embraces you with loving kindness and tender mercies; Who satisfies your old age with good things so that your youth is renewed like the eagle...God is full of compassion and gracious...For as the heaven is high above the earth, so great is His mercy toward them that revere Him. As far as the east is from the west, so far has He removed our transgressions from us. Like a father has compassion upon his children, so has God compassion upon them that revere Him. For He knows our frame, He remembers that we are dust...But the mercy of God is from everlasting to everlasting upon them that revere Him, and His righteousness unto children 's children. (Ps 113.2-3; 103.1-5, 8-18)

A PRAYER

Dear God:
   I know I should be grateful for Your many gifts. You gave me life; You endowed me with skills and a mind to think. You gave me the power of speech by which I can relate and reach out to others. Yet, I am downcast. I feel no joy. I cannot see what is good in my life. Help me, O God, to expel the demons of bitterness and sadness from my mind. Help me to recognize that which is good and be grateful for every kindness people have shown me. Give me a sense of Your nearness and enlighten me to see that my life has meaning because You created me. I bless You, O God, and seek Your presence. Amen.

7 Looking for Meaning and Purpose in Life

In T.S. Eliot's drama *The Cocktail Party*, one of the characters, Edward, tells the psychiatrist, "I am obsessed by the thought of my own insignificance." The Viennese Jewish philosopher Viktor Frankl declared that modern man is afflicted by a deep sense of meaninglessness and emptiness. This is particularly true of Americans. While 25 percent of European students suffer from a sense of meaninglessness, 61 percent of American students do so.

Whether life has any meaning or purpose is a question that challenges all of us. Every thinking person will at one time or another wonder what this life is all about. Does life make sense? Does human life have a higher purpose? What makes it more significant than the life of a cockroach? A number of thinkers and writers reached very negative conclusions about life.

Clarence Darrow, despite his brilliant success as a defense attorney, said: "Life is an awful joke."

W. Somerset Maugham said: "There is no reason for life and life has no meaning."

Shakespeare in Macbeth was contemptuous of life: "It is a tale told by an idiot full of sound and fury, signifying nothing."

Woody Allen said: "Life is a sexually transmitted disease."

Any adversity or setback, especially serious illness, will prompt you to reassess your life and career. As you take stock of hardships, sacrifices, and disappointments, you may well ask, is life worthwhile?

An old Persian story tells of a king who commissioned the wisest men of his kingdom to spend ten years studying the best books of all nations about the meaning of life. After 10 years the wise men returned with a caravan carrying 500 books. The king did not have the time to read such a library and ordered the men to come back with a condensation of those 500 books.

After 10 years his wise men returned with a single book containing a summary of all they had read. By this time the king, already old and pleading poor eyesight, asked the leader of his wise men to tell him the gist of all the books about life he had studied. The sage answered: "The gist of what we have learned is that life is to be born, to grow, to decline, and to die."

Whether human life means anything at all is a question that pops into your mind at the death of someone you care about, and you think of your own inevitable demise. Why go through an existence bound to end with decline, enfeeblement, and death?

What makes it worthwhile?

Sigmund Freud can't say anything about the meaning of life. Although an avowed atheist, he admitted that "the idea of life having a purpose stands and falls with the religious system."

It is a question for which science has no answer. Only religion says something about the meaning and purpose of life.

In Judaism, Biblical authors and rabbinical sages are split between an optimistic and a pessimistic view of life. The optimistic view is stated in the very first chapter of the Bible:

And God created man in His own image...male and female He created them. God blessed them and said: be fruitful and multiply, fill the earth and master it. (Gen. 1.27-28)

In plain words, there are two purposes to human life: first, the preservation of human kind by way of procreation; second, management of the earth. This is the strongest affirmation of purpose for human existence to be found anywhere. According to the Bible, life is not a gift but a task. Man is charged to act as God's custodian of the earth and all its creatures.

But only a couple of pages further the Bible shatters illusions of human grandeur: "Dust you are and unto dust you shall return." (Gen. 3.19)

Another Biblical book, named after its author, Kohelet, who is called by our sages *the wise man*, is more explicit in downgrading human life: "...as regards men...they are beasts....They have one and the same fate; as one dies so dies the other; man has no superiority over beast, since both amount to nothing. Both go to the same place; both come from dust and both return to dust." (Eccl. 3.18-20)

This is not an eccentric judgment but Judaism's standard view of human life expressed in a prayer of our daily morning service:

What are we? What is our life? What is our righteousness? What is our strength? What is our might?...Are not all the heroes like nothing before You, the famous as if they never existed, the wise as if devoid of wisdom?...The days of their lives are empty before You...for all is vain.

So what are we to do with our lives? Kohelet would not have you brood over man's fate. It is what it is. So, make the best of every opportunity for pleasure. Enjoy whatever you can: "eat drink and enjoy." (Eccl.5.17; 8.15) He goes on to say: Be well dressed. Try to look your best in your clothes and appearance and "enjoy life with a woman you love all the days of your life for that is your portion in this life." (Eccl. 9.9) In his next sentence Kohelet urges us to live to the fullest: "Whatever Is in your power to do, do it with all your might." (Eccl. 9.10)

Our rabbinic sages confirmed Kohelet's call for the enjoyment of life with the amazing statement that on the final Judgment Day you will be condemned for denying yourself any legitimate pleasure.

Our sages, however, would not say anything about the higher meaning and purpose of life because they did not know.

I once officiated at a wedding at which Tommy Corcoran, President Roosevelt's advisor, offered the following toast: "To the bride: try to understand your husband and love him; to the groom: love your wife but don't try to understand her."

Maybe that's the way to live. Love life, make the most of it, but don't try to understand its meaning.

Many things are unexplainable. Once when Beethoven played a new sonata for a friend, he was asked, "What does it mean?"

Beethoven returned to the piano, played the whole sonata again and said, "That's what it means." Life is what it is. If there is a higher meaning to life, we are not mentally equipped to grasp it.

During the Crimean War a British cavalry commander ordered his brigade of some 600 men to make a frontal attack against a Russian artillery battery, which completely destroyed the brigade. Alfred Lord Tennyson immortalized the case in his poem *The*

Charge of the Light Brigade, which includes these lines:

"Forward, the Light Brigade!"
....Theirs not to make reply,
Theirs not to reason why,
Theirs but to do and die.

Human life is existence under higher order. Why and what for, we do not know. We have no knowledge, only faith that our life is not pointless, not without meaning and purpose. The prophet Isaiah did not pretend to know why God created but he was certain that it was not a waste: "The Creator of heaven who alone is God, who formed the earth and made it....He created it, not a waste." (Is. 45.18) Human life is not a waste. It has a purpose, albeit beyond man's power of understanding. Our knowledge is very limited, as acknowledged by the philosopher/poet Santayana:

Our knowledge is a torch of smoky pine
That lights the pathway but one step ahead
Across a void of mystery and dread
(*The Light of Faith*)

The fact that we cannot see something doesn't mean it isn't there. The meaning of human life is part of a larger context which is beyond our comprehension. A single painted tile by itself may be meaningless. But if seen as part of a mosaic, it has meaning. We human beings are part of a larger mosaic of life, of cosmic dimensions. The fundamental fact of our existence is connection, as Shelley put it:

Nothing in the world is single
All things by a law divine
In one spirit meet and mingle
(*Love's Philosophy*, Stanza 1)

In his book *Tuesdays with Morrie,* Mitch Albom tells a story about a little wave bobbing along in the ocean, having a great time, until he noticed that the other waves were crashing against the shore. "My God, this is terrible," he said, "look what's going to happen to me!"

Another wave came along and asked, "Why do you look so sad?"

The little wave said, "You don't understand! We're all going to crash! All of us waves are going to be nothing! Isn't it terrible?"

The other wave answered, "No, you don't understand. You're not a wave—you're part of the ocean." (*Tuesdays with Morrie*, p. 73)

The meaning of our life is being part of something larger than ourselves. It is in this larger context of all things, that the unknowable purpose of our life is embedded.

Inasmuch as the purpose of life is unknowable, the psychologist Erich Fromm argued that you yourself must give purpose to your life.

Rabbi Hillel put it this way: "If I am not for myself, who will be ? And, if I am only for myself, what am I?"

Your first responsibility is to make something of yourself. You are of no use to anyone unless you develop your abilities. Only you can do that.

But a life dedicated only to its own preservation, a self-centered life, will leave you with a feeling of emptiness, the feeling that life has no purpose.

An elderly wealthy lady in deep mourning at the death of her son placed a standing order with a florist for a bouquet of flowers to be set on his grave each week. One day a chauffeur-driven car stopped at the florist's shop. The lady, frail and pale, told the florist, "My doctors tell me that I am very ill. Before I die I want to see my son's grave once more and put the flowers there myself."

The florist said, " You know, ma'am, the flowers you have me deliver every week last just a short while and nobody can enjoy them. It seems such a waste. Seeing the shocked expression on the lady's face, the florist quickly added, "Please don't misunderstand me. I belong to a visiting society. We take flowers to hospital patients, orphanages, homes for the aged. Lady, there are people there, but nobody can see your flowers at the cemetery."

The woman motioned to the chauffeur to drive on—and the florist was sorry he opened his mouth.

A few months later, he was surprised by another visit from the lady. This time she had driven herself. Turning to the florist, she said, "I now take the flowers to lonely sick people. You were right. It makes them happy and it makes me happy. The doctors can't explain my recovery. But I have now something to live for."

A sense of meaning and purpose gives life a mighty boost. The lack of meaning and purpose enfeebles you and threatens your life.

Albert Einstein, who could not find a cosmic meaning for human existence, would have agreed with Erich Fromm that we ourselves must give purpose to our lives. We gain this sense of purpose only in our relations with others. Einstein said, "The life of the individual has meaning only insofar as it aids in making the life of every living thing nobler and more beautiful....One thing we know, that we are here for the sake of others. How much our lives are built upon the labors of others....We must give in return as much as we have received."

Emily Dickinson said it poetically:

If I can stop one heart from breaking
I shall not live in vain.
If I can ease one life the aching
Or cool one pain,
...I shall not live in vain
(*If I Can Stop One Heart From Breaking*)

Our sages, urging us to help a fellowman, went as far as to say that he who saves one human being is as if he saved all mankind.

It implies that even a single act of kindness and concern for others is significant and makes a difference.

According to the essayist George Washington Burnap, purpose and happiness can be found by way of three essentials: "something to do, something to love, something to hope for." (*The Sphere and Duties of Woman: A Course of Lectures,* Lecture IV, p. 99)

We often complain about work, but having nothing to do is worse. Much of our sense of meaning and purpose is derived from work and activities. Woody Allen said that he drowns himself in work in order to distract his mind from the chilling emptiness and absurdity of human existence. A job or volunteer work will confirm your feeling that you are needed.

Among my friends are a couple of retired lawyers who spend several hours each week at the Hebrew Home conducting what they call "a schmooze group." Their discussions of current events or whatever are as stimulating to them as to their old schmooze partners.

I met a woman recently who volunteers as a mentor in weekly face-to-face sessions with a needy child. She was asked to help a girl of about 7 years who could hardly talk. After she met with the child for a number of years, the girl graduated from primary school with high marks, then distinguished herself in high school where she was chosen valedictorian of her class, and then went to college on scholarships, graduating with top honors. Helping that needy child no doubt added a sense of meaning to the woman's life.

You can give purpose to your own life by helping people in need. Our Temple journal often tells of opportunities to serve. Any kind of volunteer work, such as helping meals on wheels, staffing a soup kitchen for the poor, or reading for the blind will give you a feeling of significance and fill your life with meaning.

As for the second essential, Burnap did not say it is to be loved, but rather it is to love someone. Those who are blessed with a happy marriage and good relations with children and grandchildren see much meaning in life. Bar and Bat Mitzvah celebrations, weddings, the birth of children, birthdays, and anniversaries enrich our life. We enjoy reunions with family members, although there are exceptions, which prompted George Burns's remark: "I love my family—in another city." My late father-in-law said, "A good thing about grandchildren is that the end of the day, you can send them home."

As for the third essential, hope, choose a cause for which to work; think of ways to improve your life; help create a better community; seek ways to reduce suffering, help create peace, and work for the fulfillment of such hopes.

A purpose in life is not something that falls into your lap. It is a personal choice. Our purposes change from youth to old age and the challenge is to embrace appropriate purposes at every stage of life.

Often it is not until late in life that we recognize meaning and purpose in our existence. In retrospect, we are thankful for a good marriage, for the family we raised, for the friendships we developed, and for the achievements in our work or profession.

Like all retirees, I have since my retirement spent more time on shopping and domestic chores, some of which, to be frank, are not enjoyable. For example, taking the garbage out. Maxine tries to have me do it with enthusiasm. She hands me the trash to take out with the words, "This will add meaning to your life."

Alfred Lord Tennyson was a man of faith but was profoundly shaken by doubts, which he expressed in *In Memoriam*. We do not know the higher meaning and purpose of human life, yet we may hope there is one.

> Behold we know not anything:
> I can but trust that good shall fall
> At last—far off—at last to all,
> And every winter change to spring.
> So runs my dream, but what am I?
> An infant crying in the night;
> An infant crying for the light
> And with no language but a cry.
> (*In Memoriam* LIV.13-20)

> I stretch lame hands of faith and grope,
> And gather dust and chaff, and call
> To what I feel is Lord of all,
> And faintly trust the larger Hope.
> (*In Memoriam* LV.17-20)

8 Self-Renewal

The Nobel laureate Hermann Hesse wrote the novel *Demian*, which was sensationally popular in Europe in the early 1920s and, after its translation into English, drew an enormous readership in the United States in the 1960s. The key to its appeal was its theme: a young man trying to find himself. Those of us who have, with high hopes and great expense, sent children to college, dread to see the graduate's tormented face as he is trying to answer the question: "So, what are you going to do now?" And then comes the unnerving answer: "I need time to find myself."

"Finding yourself" isn't just a post-graduate problem.

Many of us suppressed the urge to find ourselves. As soon as we received our diplomas we went on with life, getting into our professions, switching jobs, getting married, yet wondering at times in moments of solitary reflection: Is this the life I really want? The need to find oneself doesn't disappear; it just hits you later on in life.

The key sentiment in Herman Hesse's *Demian* spoke especially to me and I suppose will speak to many as well: "The life of every person is a way to himself....No one has ever become fully himself yet all strive to be."

All of life's experiences lead to new self-knowledge. We all have some self-image we wish to realize; even if we fail to do so, it lingers in our minds.

When the Torah is returned to the Ark, we chant the words *chadesh yameynu*—"renew our days." Every day can be the time of self-renewal. Think of a new beginning in the way you spend your time, a new beginning in your marriage, how you relate to your children, your career, and the cultivation of your mind.

We all engage constantly in some kind of self-renewal: dieting, exercise, and contributing to the multibillion dollar cosmetic business to improve our appearance, or as T.S. Eliot's Alfred J. Prufrock put it, "To prepare a face to meet the faces that you meet."

On a more profound level, self-renewal is forced upon us. The psychologist Gordon Allport of Harvard University, in his study *The Individual and His Religion*, wrote a few pages which are especially relevant to the need for self-renewal. I was struck by his comparison of youth in their twenties with adults in their thirties and older. The average college graduate in his or her twenties is bursting with eagerness to try his or her own way, free of parental control and parental codes of conduct. At that point in life, the young man or woman has not yet had the rude shock that comes to nearly all adults when they first realize that their abilities are not likely to equal their aims.

It is often in the thirties and forties that one becomes realistic. Then the task of self-renewal boils down to accepting one's limitations and making the best of it. But you can't do that unless you are brutally honest with yourself. The founder of the Chassidic movement, who was known as *the Besht*, was once visited by a follower with the complaint, "I have labored hard and long in the service of God. Yet I see no improvement. I am still an ordinary and ignorant person."

The Besht answered, "You have gained the realization that you are ordinary and ignorant, and this in itself is a worthy accomplishment." An honest self-appraisal is the pre-condition for self-renewal.

In the tragedy *Hamlet*, Shakespeare admonishes us through Polonius, who says: "To thine own self be true."

This sounds like a noble motto for life, but there is a problem: Which self shall we strengthen and uphold? The human self is a composite: There is the violent self, the submissive self, the criminal self, the altruistic self, the greedy self, and the vain, self-inflating self, to mention but a few.

This suggests the major task and, I should say, the very purpose of our life: to create and maintain the best possible self and keep in check all the forces, impulses, and temptations which would degrade us. Jewish tradition is very much aware of our human corruptibility. In my daily morning prayers, there is one in which I ask God not to let us fall into the power of error, transgression, and sin, nor to let the evil inclination rule over us. We ask God to keep us far from an evil person and evil companion and help us cling to our good impulses.

We walk on the brink of evil, and every day we must strengthen ourselves in resistance to wrong doing. We are bidden to immerse ourselves daily in the study of Torah to help us make "informed" choices in life and renew that part of ourselves we may call good. This always involves the rejection and discard of that other side which stands in the way of our new vision of the kind of person we want to be.

Some surprising changes may go with such self-renewal. Who could have imagined that the former queen of the flower children of the 60s, adored by admirers and reviled by others as "radical chic," the thrice-married actress Jane Fonda, would move from far left politics to profitable body culture and to an even more profitable marriage with the multibillionaire Ted Turner. But then, after the break-up of that marriage, she turned to Christianity.

How typical is the return to religion at the final stage of life, from the 60s to the 80s and beyond? Although many elderly are seen at worship services, one must not generalize. I have known oldsters who were skeptics, even atheists. However, the stage of life we call "old age" brings us insights conducive to a religious posture in life.

Consider just one aspect of self-renewal, from childhood to old age: The will and ability to control.

As young children we submit to parental control. Then come the rebellious adolescent years in which we assert our own will in clashes with one or both parents.

As young adults, we take control of ourselves and in various ways try to control others. At times we fight to have our way because "having our way" spells freedom for us.

With maturity comes the realization of limits to our freedom and power. It becomes clear that we can't get all we want and often what we get is not what we want.

Slowly and painfully, we learn to submit to circumstances not of our choosing, to the will of others, the will of a spouse, an associate, or superior in the work place.

We come to appreciate the adage of Jewish wisdom: "Don't be like an oak tree, rigid and unbending, but rather like the willow. Comes a storm, the unbending oak tree will be overturned, but the willow will sway unharmed with the wind."

Setbacks in health and chronic illness leave us no choice but to submit to reality. Self-renewal for the elderly must begin with the acceptance of their greatly diminished power and range of control. It is only at that late stage in life that some of us realize the truth of that other morning prayer which speaks of human impotence: "What are we? What is our life? What our power, our might? The famous as though they had never been and the wise as if without knowledge?"

As bereavements, losses, and pains outweigh your pleasures, it will dawn upon you that your existence, such as it is, was not your idea but that you were put into this world by a will other than your own and under conditions not of your choosing and for a purpose you cannot fathom. You are subject to the Creator and there is no alternative to submission.

I have referred to the losing streak that goes with aging. In all fairness we should mention that at every stage of life we not only incur losses but also score gains. What are some of the compensatory gains of old age to be integrated into a new self?

It is the time to sweep out of your life trivial pursuits and re-enter the halls of learning. The journalist I. F. Stone, after his retirement in his mid-seventies, took up the study of Greek at American University so that he might read Aristotle and Plato in the original text. Mature Jewish adults throughout the world are now filling the gaps of their Jewish knowledge in classes taught by master teachers. The elderly are uniquely qualified to act as the center of their extended family whose members are scattered from coast to coast and abroad. Grandparents have the time to maintain regular contact with all the branches of the family tree and strengthen the ties that bind families together.

No matter how old you are, you are never a finished product. Life demands the constant re-making of yourself to meet new situations and needs. If there is a purpose to life, self-renewal must come close to it. For remember, you are one of a kind; God created you to become fully YOU, refined and improved, developing the best there is in you.

As a young man, Benjamin Franklin proposed a mock epitaph for his gravestone:

"The Body of B. Franklin, Printer, Like the cover of an old Book, its Contents torn out and stript of its Lettering and Gilding, Lies here...it will, as he believ'd, appear once more in a new & more perfect edition, Corrected and Amended By the Author."

Our task and purpose in life is to do the revising and correcting of the self as we go along, day by day and year by year, until God chooses to return us for new life in a new edition.

9 The Problem of Evil

A Yiddish story tells about a tailor who informs his customer who brought in a pair of pants for repair that the job would take two weeks.

"Why so long?" asked the customer. "God created the whole world in only six days, and you need two weeks to fix a pair of pants?"

"But look," answered the tailor "what a botched up job the world is!"

The tailor's remark that the world is defective is not an off-beat opinion but a leading theme in Jewish thought.

The Bible's biggest story after God's creation of the world is the chronicle of a titanic struggle against evil. Its opening drama is the corruption of man. Seduced by the snake to violate God's commandment, the first human couple is expelled from a perfect existence. The first naturally born human being, Cain, killed his brother, Abel. His descendants go from bad to worse in the course of human history.

Jewish mysticism traces the origin of evil further back to the very time of creation, when God's plan for a perfect world was spoiled by a cosmic catastrophe. Subsequently, humanity in general, and the Jewish people in particular, is charged with the responsibility of repairing the world, a concept know to us as *tikkun olam*. In every worship service, we affirm this hope in the *Alenu* prayer, that the world will be perfected under the rule of the Almighty. The messianic hope for the perfection of the world is in itself a statement of the imperfection of the world in its present condition.

You don't have to be a mystic, just a realist, to recognize profound flaws in the world which challenge our faith in God. The history of civilization reveals a frightening upward spiral of destructiveness from clubbing to stabbing to shooting to explosives to nuclear devastation and now global terrorism, which is ready to use any weapon to turn the world back into chaos.

What is happening makes people of faith ask: Where is God? Does God know? Does God care about the ordeal of the innocent?

Is God indifferent to human suffering, be it global or strictly individual?

Faith in God is the mainstream of Biblical thought, but in it are undercurrents of protest against injustice and the suffering of the innocent. Our first patriarch, Abraham, questioned God's justice when informed of the impending destruction of an entire city: "Will You, indeed, sweep away the righteous with the wicked?...Shall not the Judge of all the earth do justice?" (Gen. 18.23,25)

The classic confrontation with the problem of evil is the book of Job. Job, introduced in the book's first verse as "wholehearted and upright, God-fearing and shunning evil." (Job 1.1) demands an explanation for the suffering with which he has been afflicted. The book's 40 chapters end with God's evasive answer that the human mind is much too limited to grasp God's way of governing the universe. This inconclusive answer leaves the problem of evil an open-ended question.

Another Biblical book also wrestles with the problem of evil. It offers several explanations which may strike us as more satisfactory than the open-endedness of Job—and that is the Book of Psalms.

Though ardent believers in God, the psalmists were scandalized by the reality of evil. Boldly these psalmists protest against God's silence. Where are You? Why are You hiding Yourself?

In Psalm 42 we hear the anguished outcry of the sufferer who wonders: Where is God when one needs Him? "I will say unto God, my Rock, why have You forgotten me?" (Ps. 42.10)

We expect the Creator of the world Who has a special relationship with His human creatures to know our predicament and to act as Redeemer. The psalmists won't deny His existence, but they fault Him for turning His back on evil. Psalm 10 complains, "Why do You keep far away, O God? Why do You hide Yourself in time of trouble?" (Ps. 10.1)

Another psalmist bursts out with words that border on blasphemy: "Awake, why do You sleep, O God? Arouse Yourself....Why do You hide Your face and forget our affliction and our oppression?" (Ps. 44.24-25)

Still another psalmist, impatient with God's silence, mixes lamentation with irony: "Mine eye languishes because of affliction. I have called upon You, O God, every day. I have spread out my hands in prayer. Will You work wonders for the dead? Or, shall the shades arise and give You thanks? Shall Your mercy be proclaimed in the grave? Or, Your faithfulness in destruction?" (Ps. 88.1-13)

Having said all that, the psalmist still clings to his faith: "As for me, unto You, O God, do I cry and in the morning my prayer goes out to meet You. Why, then, do You cast me out? Why do You hide Your face from me?" (Ps. 88.14-15)

Almost amusing is the argument of Psalm 30 that God should rush to his rescue because He has nothing to gain in the death of the faithful: "What profit is there in my blood when I go down to the pit? Shall the dust praise You? Shall it declare Your truth?" (Ps. 30.10)

Far back in antiquity, in the world's most ancient mythologies, evil was understood as the work of demons, devils, or counter-gods who were hostile to life and bent upon its destruction. Monotheistic Jewish thought could not accept the existence of competitive divinities doing evil. Consequently, what is called evil must somehow be the work of the One God. Indeed, the prophet Isaiah speaks of God as the Source of both good and evil:

I am God and there is none else;
I form the light and create darkness,
I make peace, and create evil. (Is. 45.7)

The Rabbis, however, were loath to attribute evil to God and tried to explain why God would permit it. One explanation by Rabbi Nachman ben Samuel holds that what we call evil actually serves a good purpose. Without the evil urge, in the form of greed and pride, people would not engage in enterprises and strive to achieve. Without the evil urge in rivalry, people would not develop superior skills. Without lust, people would not take spouses and beget children. (Montefiore #788)

One of the greatest rabbinical sages, Rabbi Akiba, used to repeat his favorite saying, *gam zu l'tova*—"this too is for the good." A charming legend tells of problems he encountered on a journey. Unable to find lodging in a certain town, he was compelled to pass the night outside its walls. He resigned himself to this hardship. When, during the night, a lion devoured his donkey, a cat killed the rooster whose crowing was to awaken him at dawn, and the wind blew out his lamp, the only remark he made was, "This too must be for good." When morning dawned he found out how true his words had been. Armed men had entered the town and had robbed, kidnapped, and killed people. He alone escaped because the place where he had slept had not been noticed in the dark, nor had the braying of the donkey nor the crowing of the rooster betrayed his whereabouts. (*Talmud*, Ber. 60b) All his losses had been for his own good. However, not all Jews are persuaded that God allows us to suffer for our own good. Shalom Aleichem mocks this theory by having Tevye the dairyman say, "With God's help, I starve to death."

About 923-932 CE, the Muslim philosopher al-Razi wrote that life is a punishment and a great evil. Maimonides in his *Guide of the Perplexed* (Part III, Ch. 12) took sharp issue with al-Razi. He argued that the ignoramus judges everything by the way it affects him as an individual. He sees the world revolving around himself. If something contrary to his wishes happens, he judges all existence to be an evil. (Twersky, *A Maimonides Reader*, pp. 300-1) The right way to view life is to recognize that in the context of total existence, man and all the animals are nearly nothing, as it is said in Psalm 144: "Lord, what is man?...Man is like vanity," (Ps. 144.3-4) or Isaiah: "The nations are as a drop of a bucket." (Is. 40.15)

Maimonides offers his own explanation for the evils which afflict mankind (Twersky, *A Maimonides Reader*, p. 302). He states, "Most of the evils that befall the individual are his own doing and not God's, as is said in the Torah: 'Is corruption His? No! His children's is the blemish.' " (Dt. 32.15)

What evils befall us come in three categories:

- Man's physical nature begets changes and infirmities due to the law of "coming into being and passing away." The very physical changes by which a creature of flesh and blood develops also account for his demise. Moreover, mortality makes possible the regeneration of the species.

- Second are the evils we inflict upon one another through theft, oppression, and violence.

- Outnumbering all are the evils individuals inflict upon themselves through vices such as overeating, drinking, and other abuses that cause ailments.
(Twersky, A Maimonides Reader, p. 304)

Maimonides' valiant attempt to argue for the essential goodness of life left many subsequent thinkers unconvinced.

So gloomy a view is not found in the psalms. The prevailing thought is that evil can be overcome. Psalm 34 makes a point for which history provides ample illustrations: "Evil shall kill the wicked." (Ps. 34.22) Ultimately, evil is self-destructive. Did not Hitler, who turned millions of Jewish lives into ashes, die by his own hand, his remains doused with gasoline and burned exactly as were his victims?

Psalm 92 comes up with a hopeful view. God lets evil grow and fester so that He may wipe it out all at once. The psalmist puts it this way: "When the wicked spring up as the grass, and when all the workers of iniquity do nourish; it is that they may be destroyed forever." (Ps. 92.8)

We may only hope that when the atrocities of terrorism reach a new climax, the world will rally to terminate this plague once and for all.

The only trouble with this optimistic expectation of the triumph of justice is the question of timing: When will it happen? Today, many would agree with Ogden Nash's wry comment: "There has never been an era when so many things were going so right for so many of the wrong persons." (*Everybody Tells me Everything*)

An altogether different, even unique, response to the problem of evil is stated in Psalm 73. This psalmist observed with deep resentment the prosperity of evil doers, so much so that he wavered in his own faith. But one day, entering the sanctuary, he had a religious experience. It was a revelation, not of a particular commandment, not a message from God he could put into words, but the sudden realization that he was inseparable from God. It came to him in a flash that he was always in God's presence,: "I am continually with

You," he exclaimed. (Ps. 73.23). The stress is on the word "continually." He knows himself to be in God's presence, whether conscious of it or not. The assurance of God's presence outweighs all other concerns: "As for me, the nearness of God is my good. And beside You I desire nothing on earth."(Ps. 73.28)

When all is said and done, we cannot give satisfactory reasons for all the suffering and evil in life. We cannot explain it but neither can we explain the opposite, the reality of goodness, the capacity for love, the readiness to give and sacrifice for the other. The mystery of evil is offset by the mystery of good in God's world.

Is it possible that good will overcome evil? I grew up in Vienna, Austria. In the basement of our apartment building lived a young, unemployed, and unskilled drifter. My family felt sorry for him and occasionally gave him some food and odd jobs as a handyman. After the Nazi occupation of Austria, Jews were rounded up to be jailed or killed. One day our doorbell rang. I opened the door and there stood that fellow, now dressed up in a Nazi uniform. "I have an order to pick you up," he said. I looked at him; he lowered his eyes as though ashamed and then said, "Get into bed! I'll tell them that you were too sick for me to pick you up."

To this day, I wonder what moved him to spare me. Did a spark of compassion or gratitude, at least at that moment, prevail in the heart of that Nazi?

We must not underestimate the power of evil, but neither should we underestimate the redeeming power of good. The following case was reported from North Africa during the war in 1942. It involved a certain adjutant, Ernst Tessier, of the French Foreign Legion, a tight-lipped man of about 39 who did not mix with his fellow legionnaires or enjoy their choice of recreation. One day he ordered four newly enrolled Jews to report to his quarters. Their initial fear was quickly dissipated when, to their surprise, he said, "I love all Jews; I think they are the most civilized people I have met."

One night, chatting with him in his tent, they were interrupted by a new recruit. "Legionnaire Rathenau," saluted the newcomer as he gave his name. Tessier leaped from his chair. "*Rathenau* did you say? Are you related to the foreign minister of Germany?

Walther Rathenau was one of Europe's most brilliant Jewish statesmen. He organized Germany's industry in World War I and later served as Germany's foreign minister. In 1922, he was the first of our people to be assassinated by the Nazis. Over one million mourners lined the streets of Berlin for the funeral. Two of the three assassins committed suicide, and the one caught by the police got 15 years in jail.

Now, when the new legionnaire answered Ernst Tessier, "Yes, I am his nephew, sir," Tessier grew pale and said, "Rathenau, I am the man who murdered your uncle. My real name is Ernst Werner Teschow." With these words he drew from his pocket a faded scrap of paper, carefully unfolded it. It was a letter in German to Teschow's mother, written by the mother of the murdered Rathenau:

In grief unspeakable, I give you my hand, you of all women, the most to be pitied. Say to your son that in the name and spirit of him he has murdered, I forgive, even as God may forgive, if before an earthly judge he make full confession of his guilt and before the heavenly one repent. Had he known my son, one of the noblest men earth bore, he had rather have turned the weapon on himself. May these words give peace to your soul.

Mathilda Rathenau.

Tessier, now sobbing, revealed the rest of his story. Released from prison after only five years, he enlisted in the French Foreign Legion, read the writings of Rathenau, studied Jewish history, and even learned Hebrew. Said Tessier, "I discovered what barbarians the Nazis really were and so I devoted all my energies in the last 15 years to suppressing the evil in my soul, just as mother Rathenau conquered herself when she wrote this letter to my mother. In all these years I have done all I could to help the Jewish people."

Investigators verified the fact that in 1941, Tessier, disguised as a dock worker in Marseille, smuggled 700 Jews out of occupied France into freedom.

We should be appalled by the pervasive reality of evil in the world, in humans, including ourselves—but we must never lose faith in the possibllity that evil can be overcome by good, that evil doers can be rehabilitated. Remember the words spoken to Cain as he was about to murder his brother Abel: "...sin stands at the door...but you can overcome it." (Gen. 4.7)

By age-old Jewish tradition, a discourse should end on a hopeful note. I shall give two reasons for my own hope:

- The potential for good in man is every bit as real as his inclination to do evil.

- I believe that we human beings are not the only players in the shaping of our destiny. When you face problems too big for you to handle, do as the psalmist says, "Cast your burden upon God." (Ps. 55.23) That is, trust that in countless, unfathomable ways, God may help.

When some years ago I was wheeled out of the recovery room following successful surgery at Johns Hopkins hospital, I spotted a sign that read, "Good morning. This is God. I will be handling all your problems today. I will not need your help. So relax and have a good day."

Judaism's moral realism affirms that there is good and evil in man. But Jewish faith expects the good to grow stronger. Our Messianic hope is a metaphor for the power to overcome evil. The Messiah stands for the victory of good over evil. However long the delay, we still believe in the triumph of good.

10 Sin and the Devil

Life is full of contradictions. There is order, but also disorder. There are predictable developments according to laws and unpredictable random events. There is pleasure and pain, growth and decay, disease and healing, life and death.

To the rationalists of two centuries ago, the world looked like a machine. I see it as a gigantic stomach, nature feeding on itself. Bernard Berenson must have seen it that way too when he remarked, "Life is at the expense of others." Whatever grows out of nature is consumed and recycled—for what purpose, no one knows.

One of the fundamental differences between man and other animals is that man is the only species that can think about himself and exert a measure of control over his instincts. Man is the only creature with a sense of right and wrong.

In the course of the last 100,000 years, our skills have widened the gap between us and all other animals. We have grown in the capacity for cooperation, for love, for helpfulness, for giving of ourselves, for creativity—capacities we call *good*. But we have not lost our capacity for hurting, hating, and destroying, capacities we call *evil*.

If we see in our good qualities a reflection of God's attributes, as is suggested in the Biblical statement that God created us in His own image (Gen. 1.27), the question arises: whence come those qualities we call evil? Are those also a reflection of God's attributes? Or do we owe those to some demon in the universe, a kind of anti-God? Or is there in man an innate will or drive to do evil—something called *sin*?

What is sin? As commonly understood, sin is a corruption in human nature, a propensity for going astray, for acting contrary to the will of God. This was the consensus among Jews and Christians until the l8th century. Then the rationalists and skeptics of the Enlightenment (1650s to the 1780s) undertook to blow away what they considered to be the cobwebs of superstition. Sin was either exposed as the invention of a crafty priesthood by which to keep the masses in line or reduced to a synonym for error or mistake.

Do we have a different understanding of sin?

Let us admit that for many of us sin has become a rather meaningless term. It no longer carries that solemn and frightening connotation of an offense against God. We now use the word casually, like in the cartoon I saw of a little girl saying her nightly prayer, "And please God forgive the dessert Grandma had at the restaurant. She said it was sinful."

Who was it that took the sting out of sin?

In one of the great intellectual revolutions of all time, Jean Jacques Rousseau, in the middle of the l8th century, led us into a new estimate of man which did away with the whole idea of sin. At the age of 29, Rousseau arrived in Paris where he was shocked by the artificiality and unfairness of society. Embittered, he wrote his famous *Social Contract*. Some of its statements became the revolutionary slogans of the century, such as "Man is born free, but everywhere he is in chains" or the phrase "the noble savage." Rousseau argued that man is naturally good but corrupted by social institutions. Therefore, society is in need of change, an idea which stoked the fires of the French Revolution.

If Rousseau returned to the scene today, he would find society radically altered, with material comforts unimaginable in his time now available, the blight of illiteracy and the scourge of famine eliminated in the Western world, and the normal life-span more than doubled. Yet, with all of this social progress, has man reached the perfection of which Rousseau held him capable? Why do we lock our doors? Why do we protect our buildings, including churches and synagogues, with security systems? Why do we press for more policemen on the beat? Why don't we trust human nature?

The optimistic assessment of man's noble nature is contradicted by a more realistic estimate derived from experience. There is overwhelming evidence of our moral deficiencies. We have good reason to be afraid of our fellow man. Despite all material improvements, we have an unimproved humanity.

Someone said, "The caveman has not disappeared. He has learned to wear a tuxedo."

In the l9th century, Horace Mann in Boston offered a cure for crime: education. Build more schools. We have done so, only to find our schools infested with violence and the nation's prisons overcrowded. One out of every 200 citizens is serving time as a convict. When Hitler seized power, Germany was probably the best educated nation of Europe. It had the largest number of scholars and scientists. Superior knowledge, however, did not produce superior morality.

Was there something wrong with Rousseau's and Horace Mann's basic theses? Why does not man's natural goodness assert itself? What is the obstacle?

Many of us still hesitate to call it sin.

Upon seeing wrong or misconduct in a man or woman, we blame it on psychological or environmental problems. Anti-social behavior, infidelity, lying, and stealing are explained as the result of emotional immaturity, neurosis, faulty toilet training, and a string of psychological problems—but not moral problems.

William Allingham suggested the moral evasion with the verse:

Sin we have explained away;
Unluckily, the sinners stay.

We have found new labels for the old evils. Why all this verbal masquerade? I'll tell you what we are trying to hide: responsibility! Nobody should get the blame. We are resisting accountability. It is escapism. To blame our calamities on others is second nature with us. It has been said that every man needs a wife because a lot of things go wrong which you can't blame on the government.

People will come up with the most incredible excuses. An 88-year-old man in Oklahoma City who was driving a motor scooter without a license explained his misdeed to the traffic court: "I did not apply for a license because I thought you had to be accompanied by a parent."

We blame our troubles on others. What's wrong with the world? The leaders, the statesmen, the diplomats, the parents, the teachers—it's always *they*, those others, who are making trouble. Anna Russell put it in these words:

At three I had a feeling of
Ambivalence toward my brothers,
And so it follows naturally
I poisoned all my lovers.
But now I'm happy, I have learned
The lesson this has taught;

That everything I do that's wrong
Is someone else's fault.

One of America's wisest old men was Judge Learned Hand. Shortly before his death at 89 years, he gave an interview in which he discussed William Shirer's book *The Rise and Fall of the Third Reich.* "What did you think of the history of Nazism," asked the reporter. Judge Hand stared into space to do some thinking and then said, "You know, the trouble is that it isn't just the Nazis. It isn't just the Russians. It's human nature. Human nature through the centuries."

So, the problem is our defective and delinquent human nature.

The Harvard-trained psychiatrist Karl Menninger was quite specific. In 1972, this highly respected scientist and founder of the renowned Menninger Clinic of Topeka, Kansas, published a landmark book with a title that shocked many of his colleagues: The title was *Whatever Became of Sin?* In it he had this to say: "For some, the aggressiveness, selfishness, greediness, destructiveness, ruthlessness, and pride of our fellow travelers are but expressions of our humanity. And why apologize for it? 'Need we be ashamed of being human?' they ask. That's the way we are, and let there be no reproaches, no regret, guilt, depression, repentance, responsibility. Begone such words as *sin*." (p. 191)

"But," says Menninger, "the time has come for scientists to reconsider" the old notion of sin "and give it an appropriate place in their work." (p. 191)

Menninger clinches his point with a proposal by the historian Arnold Toynbee "to establish more firmly in national, international, and personal affairs the supreme importance of distinguishing right from wrong, to end the concealment of sin under various euphemistic disguises, but to confess it and atone for it and desist from it." (p. 192).

Now, let us consider a Jewish understanding of sin. The word "sin" appears in the Bible for the first time in connection with Cain's intention of murdering his brother Abel. He was envious because preference had been shown to Abel's offering.

God said, "Why are you angry? Why is your face fallen? If you do right, you will be uplifted, but if you do not right, sin couches at the door. Its urge is toward you, yet you can master it." (Gen. 4.5-7)

The phrase "sin couches at the door" suggests two possible interpretations of sin: first, that sin is some sort of demonic being waiting to seduce Cain. Or, the phrase may be understood as a graphic way of saying, "Watch out, Cain, you are very close to sinning. You have the urge, but you can master it."

The latter is the preferred Jewish understanding. Sin is not a demon outside of us, but an ever-present tendency which we can control. We can master it.

But it is a struggle as tough as warfare. Said Ben Zoma, "Who is mighty? He who subdues his *yetzer*, that is, urge, impulse, or inclination, as is written in Proverb 16, line 32: He who is slow to anger is better than the mighty, and he that rules his spirit than he that conquers a city." (*Talmud*, Pirke Avot 4.1)

How do you keep yourself morally clean?

The rabbis had no illusion. Every person is a life-time battlefield between two contradictory urges, the *yetzer ha-ra* (evil urge) and the *yetzer ha-tov* (good urge). There is no final victory. However, there is help.

The Talmud tells us: "God says to the Israelites, I created within you the evil *yetzer*, but I created the Torah as an antidote. As long as you occupy yourselves with Torah, the *yetzer* will not rule over you." (*Talmud*, Kid. 30b, as quoted by Montefiore #762)

By Torah is meant not just the text but living the disciplined life of obedience to its commandments and prohibitions as interpreted by the sages and rabbis during the last 2000 years. This is made clear in one of our oldest daily morning prayers of Talmudic origin which, in addition to Torah, refers to another source of help in our struggle for moral integrity:

O God and God of our ancestors, train us in your Torah and make us cling to Your commandments. Lead us not into sin, transgression, iniquity, temptation, or disgrace. Let not the evil urge rule over us. Keep us far from a bad man and a bad companion; make us cling to *yetzer ha-tov*, the good urge, and to good works. Subdue our inclination so that it may serve you.

Never, never think you are above temptation. They tell of Rabbi Amram, known as "the pious," who gave temporary shelter on the upper floor of his house to a group of women who had been liberated from captivity. For their safety, the ladder leading to the room was removed. A ray of light fell on one of the scantily dressed women who was walking back and forth near the window. Rabbi Amram, overcome by lust, dragged the extremely heavy ladder to the house and when he had climbed half-way up, he suddenly stopped and shouted, "Amram's house is on fire." People rushed to his place but saw no fire. Then the rabbis came and said, "You frightened us by a false alarm." He replied, "It is better that you should be falsely alarmed about my house than that you should be ashamed of Amram." Then, the story goes, something like a flash of fire issued forth from him. It was the evil urge and Amram said, "You are fire and I am flesh, but I am stronger than you." (*Talmud*, Kid. 81a, as quoted by Montefiore #770)

So far, we have dealt only with man's responsibility for evil—what about God's accountability for creating a world flawed by evil? Should not a perfect and all powerful God have been able to create a human race incapable of committing evil? Could God not have created human beings immune to sin?

God has some defenders. Rabbi Nahman ben Sh'muel more than 1500 years ago argued that there is a good side to the evil urge, which was created by God together with the good urge. "Were it not for the evil urge, man would not build a house, or take a wife, or beget a child, or engage in business, as it says, 'all labor and skillful work comes of a man's rivalry with his neighbor.'" (*Midrash*, Bereshit Rabbah 9.7, as quoted by Montefiore, #788)

Lust, ambition, greed, and other components of the evil urge should not be eliminated but properly channeled so as to encourage procreation, family life, and achievements, which make up civilization.

However, that answer did not go over well with other sages who had the audacity of holding God to account for the world's defects. A Midrash (*Midrash*, Exodus Rabbah 46.4) puts it this way: "Israel complained to God: If a potter leaves a pebble in the clay and the jar leaks, is not the potter responsible? You have left in us the evil urge. Remove it, and we shall do Your will. God replied: This I will do in time to come."

One of these bold critics, Rabbi Aibu, even put a confession in God's mouth: "God said, 'I made a mistake that I created the evil urge in man, for had I not done so, he would not have rebelled against me.'" (*Midrash*, Bereshit Rabbah 27.4, as quoted by Montefiore #778)

Possibly, God might have created a different kind of a world, or, for that matter, He might not have created anything. There is no alternative to the world such as it is.

The literary critic Margaret Fuller, in a moment of resignation, exclaimed, "I accept the universe," which prompted Carlyle's dry comment, "By God, she'd better!"

Life with all of its pains and troubles is hardly a gift for our pleasure. It is more like a task thrust upon us by God for a purpose unknown, as Rabbi Elazar Ha-Kappar said so bluntly: "Regardless of your will, you were formed; regardless of your will, you were born; regardless of your will, you live; and regardless of your will, you must die." (*Talmud*, Pirke Avot. 4.29)

Our being alive is not our idea but God's to serve His purpose.

The great rival academies of Hillel and Shammai debated for two and a half years whether it would have been better if man had or had not been created. Finally, they agreed that it would have been better had man not been created, but since he has been created, let him examine what he is to do. (*Talmud*, Eruv. 13b, as quoted by Montefiore #1512)

The human task is to bow to life under terms not of our making. Therefore we must obey the laws by which our Maker would have us live.

For reasons unknown, we were given the freedom of will to choose our way or God's way. Equally inscrutable is our endowment with two contradictory impulses, the *yetzer ha-ra* and the *yetzer ha-tov.*

By whatever system of government we are governed, the quality of life will be determined by the way each of us is able to govern himself. It is safe to predict that as long as the human race will endure, man will have to wage a civil war within—the struggle between good and evil:

Here, a little child I stand
Lifting up my eager hand,
One is dirty, one is clean
I am the problem in between.
(parody of Robert Herrick's *A Child's Grace*)

What if the problem is not "in between," not inside of man, but outside of man? Could there be a cosmic force for evil which rivals God or is His equal? Zoroastrianism, the ancient Persian religion of which there are still some small remnants left in Asia, holds the dualistic faith in two gods, the good god of light and the evil god of darkness. They are in perpetual conflict, wrestling for the soul of man.

Zoroastrianism may have made some inroads in Biblical Judaism, or its main idea emerged in a different mythological scenario, the myth of the fallen angels, alluded to in Genesis: "And it came to pass...that the sons of God saw the daughters of men that they were beautiful; and they took them as wives." (Gen. 6.1-2) Out of those unions, we are told, a mighty race emerged which soon became notorious in their wickedness, which brought God to the decision of wiping them out in the flood of Noah.

This myth of the fallen angels grew immensely in the apocryphal literature which was excluded from the Hebrew Bible. In the Book of Enoch and other apocryphal books, we are told of a rebellion up in heaven led by the arch-angel Lucifer, who is identical to Satan. God crushed the rebellion and expelled Lucifer to Hell, which is the main plot of Milton's classic *Paradise Lost*. Lucifer or Satan is a major player in the New Testament, a kind of anti-God, the perpetual seducer and destroyer of man. The names Lucifer and Satan occur dozens of times in the New Testament. In sharp contrast, the Hebrew Bible mentions Satan in only two places. In the Book of Zachariah 3.1 and in the Book of Job 1.6-13, 2.1-7, Satan is mentioned in a few lines, not as God's adversary but as His employee. Satan acts as a kind of roving investigator and prosecuting attorney under God's jurisdiction. Mainstream Judaism rejected the idea of an all-powerful Satan that would diminish the majesty of God. However, in Jewish folk religion, which is often steeped in superstition, Satan is an evil demon always waiting to seduce you or pounce on you to do you harm.

This theme is captured in the novels of Isaac Bashevis Singer. They tell the story of Satan complaining to God that there isn't any work for him and he is bored.

God says, "What's the matter, why don't you do your job trying to lead people into sin?"

"Lead people into sin? Why, before I get a chance to do so, they are already sinning."

After all is said and done to raise our consciousness of sin, we must not become obsessed by it. The Chassidic Rebbe Yitzhak Meir of Ger (1799-1866) once said in a sermon, "He who talks about sin and reflects on the evil he has done is thinking evil, and what one thinks, therein is one caught. Sweep filth this way or that, and it remains filth—only the broom gets dirtier. In the time I brood over sin, I could be stringing pearls for the joy of heaven. This is what is written in Psalm 34: 'Depart from evil and do good.' (Ps. 34.15) Turn wholly away from evil, do not brood over it, but do good. You have done wrong? Then, balance it by doing right!"

11 The Dr. Jekyll and Mr. Hyde in Each of Us

In the year 1886, Robert Louis Stevenson wrote a gripping psychological allegory which has terrifying relevance to the human condition. *The Strange Case of Dr. Jekyll and Mr. Hyde* tells of a respected physician in London who had overcome certain evil inclinations in his youth to turn into a kindly, decent man. During experiments with drugs, the doctor happens to produce one which enables him to change his appearance to that of a repulsive dwarf, the embodiment of evil, whom he calls Mr. Hyde. With a similar dose, he can revert to the personality of the benevolent doctor. I won't go into the details of the story, which must be familiar, I am sure, to most of you, except for the conclusion: after changing his identity several times, doing good in the form of Dr. Jekyll and evil as Mr. Hyde, the drug loses its potency; he commits a brutal murder as Mr. Hyde, and unable to return to his former self, he commits suicide.

Stevenson may well have gotten the idea for his bizarre story from Goethe's classic drama *Faust,* whose hero, unable to reconcile his inner conflicts, exclaims, "Two souls, alas, dwell in my breast."

Stevenson's story is a parable of human nature with its fateful contradictions of good and evil impulses, tender love convertible into the will to murder. But is not the notion of a murderer within each of us a wild exaggeration? In an interview with Agatha Christy, whose dramatic output topped all records, the conversation turned to marriage. There had been some ups and downs, she admitted.

"Did you ever think of divorcing your husband?"

"Divorce," she said, "never, but murder, yes."

Very few who resent, despise, or hate someone would actually plot the murder of that person, but would go so far as to wish him dead.

The human soul is torn by a civil war: good and evil wrestle within us from earliest childhood on. Just watch a playground. For a while, the sweet little children play happily together, but any moment one will beat upon another, and if the kid could, might kill him.

Romantic lovers are shocked to discover drastic mood changes in their sweethearts; love seems to vanish in an outburst of nastiness. Nearly every married couple passes through a crisis in which one or both tearfully wonder, what has come over my partner?

"What is man?" is not just an academic question for anthropologists and theologians. If we need to get along with any other person, if we want to be more understanding as marriage partners and more effective as parents and educators and better comprehend social relationships and political behavior, we must have a realistic understanding of human nature.

The will to hurt and destroy is the most important underlying cause for war which has the potential of exterminating all human life. Our security, our survival hinges on our ability to tame the beast in man and curb his capacity for destruction.

The issue before us is: how do we cope with the contradictions inherent in human nature? What must be done to suppress and control man's evil impulse and what can be done to magnify his potential for good?

Before we attempt to cope with our evil impulse, we must ask ourselves: how did we get to be that way? There are as many answers as there are different religions and schools of philosophy and psychology. I shall single out the Biblical view which has dominated Western culture and is still echoed by many modern thinkers.

After the deluge, God decides never again to destroy all life because of sinful man. God takes some responsibility for having created man the way he is. In the words of the Bible, "man is evil from his youth." (Gen. 8.21)

The rabbis explain: The human being is born with a *yetzer ha-ra,* the evil urge. Only at the age of 13 does he develop the *yetzer ha-tov,* the good urge. It does not grow naturally. It is acquired by steady cultivation through education, discipline, wholesome association, and good examples (see *Midrash,* Bereshit Rabbah 9.7). The point is that raw human nature is not benevolent. John Stuart Mill in his essay *Nature* wrote that nature "impales men, breaks them as if on the wheel, casts them to be devoured by wild beasts, burns them to death... starves them with hunger, freezes them with cold...and has hundreds of other hideous deaths in reserve." He further observed that there is no evidence of mercy or justice in nature. What is most evident is "that a large proportion of all animals pass their existence in torment-ing and devouring other animals."

Tennyson summed it up in six words: "Nature, red in tooth and claw."

So, back to the first question I raised a while ago: What can be done to tame the evil urge which comes to us so naturally? How can we avoid causing or suffering harm?

In every relationship, parent-child, husband-wife, friendship, work, or business there must be rules. As "good fences make good neighbors," so red lines and limits one must not cross make for toler-able relationships. Total liberty to do as one pleases is intolerable. People living together in any kind of community must have their freedom limited, as the poet Louis Ginsberg said so well:

Only in fetters is liberty
Without its banks
Can a river be?

At the time when Romans ruled Judea with an iron hand and Jewish rebels plotted to overthrow the hated government, Rabbi Hanina, a leader of the peace party, pleaded, "Pray for the welfare of the ruling power, since but for the fear of it, men would swallow each other alive." (*Talmud*, Pirke Avot 3.2)

How quickly anarchy brings out the savage in human beings was shown again in Iraq by all the looting and mayhem during the short hiatus of authority after the fall of Sadam Hussein.

What happened bore out Machiavelli's warning: "It is necessary... to presuppose that all men are evil and that they are always going to act according to the wickedness of their spirits whenever they have free scope."

The founders of our Republic had no illusions about mankind. Alexander Hamilton declared before the Constitutional Assembly in 1787: "Take mankind in general. They are vicious."

John Jay, president of the Continental Congress, wrote to George Washington: "The mass of men are neither wise nor good." (June

27,1786)

Good-natured, corpulent Alexander Woolcott agreed: "All things I really like to do are either immoral, illegal, or fattening."

The world's most optimistic nation, America, long cherished the notion that more and higher education will eradicate evil. "What we call evil is simply ignorance," said Henry Ford.

The bitter lesson of the Holocaust has taught us otherwise. Europe's best educated nation, Germany, was not restrained by education from turning savage. If the Holocaust is to teach us anything, it is that knowledge does not equal higher morality. Then what does?

The first of the 150 psalms spells out in a few words the Biblical strategy for overcoming the *yetzer ha-ra,* the evil urge, and strengthening the *yetzer ha-tov,* the good urge:

Happy is the person who has not walked in the counsel of
   the wicked,
Nor stood in the way of sinners,
Nor sat in the seat of the scornful.
But his delight is in the Torah of God
And in it does he meditate day and night.

Morality has to be cultivated in human nature through steady indoctrination and right association. Note: association comes first. "Happy is the person who has not walked in the counsel of the wicked." Avoid contact with morally defective persons. Seek the company of the good and the wise. The Talmud says: If you walk into a tannery, you'll come out smelling bad. But if you step into a perfumery, even if you do not buy anything, you'll take with you some of the good fragrance of the place.

Apply that to your stepping into a house of worship. Even if you are a skeptic and don't "buy" the beliefs conveyed in some of the prayers, you will benefit in a subtle way from the reverence and spirituality of the environment.

The second point made in Psalm 1 is the stress on the Torah in which the psalmist takes delight. "In it meditate day and night." To be effective, it has got to be more than a casual and sporadic reading. For Bible reading to penetrate the debris of trivia which blocks our mind, we need to do our Torah study with intense concentration and continuity and to internalize its teachings, preferably in the stimulating company of other learners.

Unlike any other reading, most every word of the Torah is a call to action. The Torah speaks to us in terms of commandments. The *mitzvot* translate beliefs into a way of life, not in isolation but in community.

But note: a study of ethics will not make you an ethical person unless you practice habitually the values you verbalize. When Israel accepted the Torah at Mt. Sinai, they said *na-aseh v'nishma—* "we shall do and obey." The doing comes first, and then the beliefs and reasons for doing.

Aristotle, who gave the highest priority to ideas, stressed action above doctrine in moral education: "The virtues we develop by doing the acts....People come to be builders by building; harp players by playing on the harp; exactly so, by doing just actions we come to be just." (*Nichomean Ethics*)

If the bad news is man's deeply rooted impulse for evil, the good news is our mysterious capacity for good. Goodness, as we have pointed, out is not inherent in nature. It is an artificial product, something we develop out of something that comes to us from a source other than nature. Perhaps the most dramatic manifestation of the good urge is the act of repentance. People can and do change. Sinners can turn into saints. Yom Kippur is our celebration of the human capacity for change, for reform and renewal.

It may be difficult this year to be a radiant optimist but we must not drown in the flood of bad news and swallow a lopsided view of human nature. The dismal recital of evil can be matched by an honor roll that records amazing acts of human goodness. After decades of secrecy and silence, we hear more and more about the righteous gentiles who risked their lives in rescuing Jews during the Holocaust.

Best known is the story of the French Protestant village of Le Chambon whose 3,500 inhabitants saved the lives of 6,000 Jews, mostly children whose parents had been deported and murdered. They hid these children in their own houses and in dwellings built just for that purpose.

Or, take the case of Wladislaw Bartoszewski, twice Polish

foreign minister, who in 1942 risked his life and organized the underground Zogota operation specifically for the rescue of Jews. The operation saved 4,000 Jews, including 2,500 children, helping them escape and providing forged documents, shelter, and food.

A Holocaust film was made in Whitwell, Tennesee, counting no more than 1600 souls. A few years ago the principal of its middle school was shocked to learn about the Holocaust. In the course of her research she came across a Norwegian anti-Nazi symbol showing a paperclip across a swastika. That inspired the paperclip project. After teaching all classes about the Holocaust, she proposed to collect 6 million paperclips in memory of the murdered Jews The children responded with enthusiasm, wrote letters to people all over the world and ended up with a collection of 25 million paperclips and the donation of a German cattle car that had been used for death camp transports. They converted the wagon into a mini-Holocaust museum which was solemnly dedicated by all the townspeople and children. There is a footnote: There is not a single Jew in Whitwell nor did any live there in the past.

What are some of the practical applications of our inquiry into human nature?

- Be mindful of everyone's capacity for evil and scale down your expectations of people. Don't be utterly surprised if a loving and beloved person at times turns hateful and repulsive. Expect less and you will spare yourself the pain of disillusionment.

- Don't assume that a highly intelligent person is also of superior moral quality. The most brilliant are capable of great cruelty. By the same token, the simplest can be the kindliest person.

- On the other hand, no one is beyond redemption. Even the vilest can redeem himself. Ben Azzai is quoted in Pirke Avot: "Despise no man, and deem nothing impossible, for there is not a man that has not his hour, and there is not a thing that has not its place." (*Talmud*, Pirke Avot 4.2)

I'd like to illustrate this statement with a newspaper report about a man who died in Medford, Oregon, at the age of 87. Wesley Howard was reputed to be the meanest man in the county. He used to chase children off his 68 acre farmland with shotgun in hand. After his death it was revealed that he bequeathed his entire estate, worth over $11 million, to create a youth sports park on his land. So, the one believed to hate children turned out to be their generous benefactor.

Even more surprising, in the sense of an unexpected transformation, is the case of Madonna, the longtime symbol of sex and vulgarity. She has become a devotee—perhaps not permanently—of Jewish Kabbalah mysticism with a serious concern about spirituality.

Her newest book, *The English Roses,* is an illustrated book of children's stories, inoffensive by the standards of the strictest yeshiva or monastery. Proceeds from sales go to the Spirituality-for-Kids Foundation of Los Angeles, which operates camps and programs for adults and children, including the Kabbalah Children's Academy.

We must not rush to judgment about a person's character. The best may have an evil streak and the worst some hidden goodness. As Ben Azzai said, "Deem nothing impossible." If you cannot believe that goodness might assert itself against all odds in the very person who offended you, you'll find it difficult to forgive.

Having spent all this time considering the good and evil urges, I must confess my own puzzlement over this question: If God is our all-wise and all-powerful Creator, could He not have rendered us so benign as to be incapable of evil? I found my query well expressed by Sue Monk Kidd in her book *The Secret Life of Bees*:

> If I ever managed to get to heaven after everything I'd done, I hope I would get just a few minutes for a private conference with God. I want to say: Look, I know you meant well creating the world and all, but how could you let it get away from you like this? How come you couldn't stick with your original idea of paradise? People's lives are a mess. (p. 171)

The rabbis acknowledge that God allowed evil to come into

being but they assure us that He also prepared a remedy for every ill. As Ben Azzai said, everything is possible—even the day when evil will be overcome. It is the messianic hope. Dare we hope it in view of the mounting perils to human life and the succession of historic catastrophes of ever greater magnitude? Could there be a yet unimaginable outpouring of the power for good, sufficient to overwhelm evil? Can we share the hope Alfred Lord Tennyson voiced in his poem below?

The Larger Hope

O yet we trust that somehow good
Will be the final goal of ill.
To pangs of nature, sins of will,
Defects of doubt, taints of blood

That nothing walks with aimless feet;
That not one life shall be destroyed,
Or cast as rubbish to the void,
When God has made the pile complete.

Behold, we know not anything:
I can but trust that good shall fall
At last-far off-at last, to all,
And every winter change to spring.

So runs my dream; but what am I?
An infant crying in the night
An infant crying for the light
And with no language but a cry

I stretch lame hands of faith and grope,
And gather dust and chaff, and call
To what I feel is Lord of all,
And faintly trust the larger hope.

12 The Crisis of Aging

I was standing at an airport bookshop, browsing through books, when a title caught my eye: *The Joys of Aging*. Just then they announced the boarding of my flight, so I bought the book without even looking through it, rushed to the gate, boarded the plane, and took my seat, eager to read about the joys of aging. To my surprise, all pages were blank.

Ever since I have been trying to fill some of those blank pages. What could I say? Are there joys in aging and what might those be?

Ever since my retirement some 30 years ago, I have been exploring the promised land of longevity. Although the majority opinion about old age is grim and repellent, I do have some good things to say about it.

When Charles Darwin began to think about marriage he divided a sheet of paper into two sections: "MARRY" and "NOT MARRY." Under the first heading, he noted that a wife is "a friend in old age, better than a dog."

In the second column he listed counter arguments, "perhaps quarreling and less money for books" and so forth.

Using Darwin's method, I am looking at the pros and cons of age.

The column of negatives is quickly filled up.

We live in a youth-enamored culture whose sentiment was expressed by Shakespeare in a brief line: "Age, I do abhor thee; youth, I do adore thee." (*The Passionate Pilgrim*, XII)

The philosopher Seneca, called aging "an incurable disease."

The novelist Philip Roth called it "a massacre."

T.S. Eliot, in *The Love Song of Alfred J. Prufrock*, drew a pathetic picture of an old man's self-doubt and insecurity:

> I grow old....I grow old
> I shall wear the bottoms of my trousers rolled.
> Shall I part my hair behind?
> Do I dare to eat a peach?

The poet Yeats was brutal in his depiction of the elderly:

> An aged man is but a paltry thing
> A tattered coat upon a stick
> (*Sailing To Byzantium*)

Dylan Thomas was enraged:

> Old age should burn and rave at close of day
> Rage, rage against the dying of the day.
> (*Do Not Go Gentle Into That Good Night*)

It is an impotent rage, for aging cannot be arrested. We have a dilemma, as Benjamin Franklin said:

> All would live long, but none would be old.

Does old age have compensations ? What are those compensations? When I first read Robert Browning's line:

> Grow old along with me,
> The best is yet to be
> (*Rabbi Ben Ezra*)

I questioned it as poetic license. Now, a quarter century after retirement, I recognize six reasons to support Robert Browning's positive view of old age.

First is the gain of tranquility. All the important decisions have been made in earlier years. I have wrestled with my vocational choice, searched for a spouse, created a home, raised children, established myself in my career, and I no longer have a need to prove myself. I have walked the walk and had my failures and successes; all the pressures have eased, I am more relaxed than ever, I take my afternoon naps, and what a joy it is to find empty pages on my calendar showing nothing to do.

A second gain was defined by Plato more than two millennia ago: the cooling of passion. You might call it the doctrine of insignificance. If a matter is not truly significant or important, don't fret, don't worry, don't get yourself worked up. Ignore it! We get less frantic, less pushy in advanced age. Sean O'Casey wrote in his eighties: "One likes to sit back and let the world turn by itself without trying to push it."

Age does not render us indifferent to the ills of society, to the suffering and unhappiness of people around us. But, there is a "but." Clarence Darrow said it well: "At 20, a man is full of fight and hope. He wants to reform the world. When he is 70, he still wants to reform the world, but he knows that he cannot do it."

The experience of a long life teaches us that not all problems can be solved, and certainly not by ourselves. There is no quick fix for the world's economic crises. The politics of the Middle East will fester for a long time to come. Likewise, some of our intimately personal problems have no solution. All we can and must do is endure, which we are better able to do in old age than in our younger years.

The third gain that comes with old age is the art of submission. The poet Anne Marx learned it when undergoing cancer treatment: "The force beyond," she wrote, "was now in charge of my fate. I had become a submitter."

There are situations in life you cannot control. You must submit, let go, accept the unalterable. If you cannot change a health, family, or financial problem, change your attitude. Stop fighting!

Accept what must be—and, strangely, this kind of surrender to the unchangeable is conducive to peace of mind.

The fourth gift of old age is liberation from the urge to correct everyone else.

I no longer look to win every argument. The intensity of your conviction is no proof that you are right.

More often than before, it occurs to me that I might be wrong, that I don't have all the answers. I have to listen more and talk less. I am less dismissive of opinions I disagree with, more willing to consider the merits of the other side. Shall I say it marks a growth, however modest, of humility?

The fifth dividend of old age is greater appreciation and gratitude. I have become more appreciative of friendships. More often than before I keep in touch with old friends and reach out to new, especially younger people—and at my age, that means just about everyone else. I take to heart Samuel Johnson's remark at 75: "I look upon every day to be lost in which I do not make a new acquaintance."

In response to all the bad news in the world, I make a deliberate effort to be thankful for small favors, the courteous driver, the bank teller's cheerful greeting, the mail carrier's conscientiousness, the kindness of good neighbors, and my doctor's prompt response to my call. I have discovered the truth of the opening words of Psalm 92: *tov l'hodot*—"It is good to give thanks." Giving thanks is the most effective mood-changer, the best antidote to cynicism and pessimism!

Earlier in life, with many years to look forward to, I felt like a millionaire in time, spending and wasting it freely. Now that my supply of time has shrunk, I appreciate far more each day, each hour, every bit of new knowledge, and every moment with people I care for.

The sixth and most important gain is more involvement with three generations of my family, children, grandchildren, and great grandchildren. Best of all is my love affair with a married woman, Maxine, my wife, my severest critic and unfailing support in over 70 years of marriage. What a blessing to be together much of each day. I say of Maxine as did Akiba about his beloved Rachel: *mah ani, shelah*—"Whatever I am, I owe to her."

Clearly, there is a debit side to old age. With the loss of youth much else is lost. We cannot prevent physical decline though some are in denial, like Mark Twain in old age, who insisted that his memory was not failing: "I remember everything, whether it happened or not."

Our son-in-law David had a comforting word for memory loss: "If you can't remember, just forget about it!"

Do I think of death? Who does not? Of course, I do, but differently from the way I thought about it earlier in my life:

In childhood, death was a frightening monster.

In youth, death was something that happened to others, not me.

In middle-age, I wrestled intellectually with the fact of death and tried to understand it, but without conclusions.

In old age, I've given up the effort to comprehend death. I can no more understand the reason for death than for life.

More than ever I am amazed. My dominant mood is a sense of wonder at existence. I feel tossed into life by another power, by a will other than my own.

Why are we put into this life? What is it all about? Obviously, life was not created for our happiness. Then, what is its purpose? Why must life be so uncertain and on the brink of extinction?

I imagine God answering, "Who are you to make demands? Life is not an entitlement. You are here because I put you there, and you must live on whatever terms I set for your existence. I love you in my own way which is not necessarily the way you want to be loved."

We are full of unanswered questions, the most perplexing of which is, what is the point of it all? To be human is forever wondering: Why?

One thing is clear. Isolated from others, from family, friends, and the community, the individual is nothing. Each of us is the biological extension of our parents, our people, and ultimately of the first form of created life. The mystics tells us that we are even extensions of the Creator, of God Himself.

The Viennese poet Richard Beer-Hofmann expressed our absolute connectedness:

We are but riverbeds. Through you and me
Runs the blood of the past to those who shall be.
(*Lullaby for Miriam*)

The meaning of life is in our connectedness. Our purpose is inseparable from the larger purpose of the universe, which is beyond our understanding.

Old age has compensations. The Italian Jewish neurologist and Nobel laureate Rita Levi-Montalcini, in an interview on her 100th birthday, talked about the latest period of her life as the best.

We should think about aging not as falling into a dark pit but as shifting into a different stage of life with its distinctive assets and liabilities. The same idea is suggested by the following irreverent poem:

> King David and King Solomon
> Led merry, merry lives
> With many, many lady friends
> And many, many wives
> But when old age crept over them
> With many, many qualms,
> King Solomon wrote the Proverbs
> And King David wrote the Psalms
> (James Ball Naylor)

As for death, I reject the term "departure." We are not departing; we are not going anywhere; we're staying in God's world, and forever connected with our Maker. It is my leap of faith. In that faith, I recite each night Psalm 31, verse 6:

> *B'yado afkid ruchi, beyt ishan v'a-eera*
> *V'im ruchi geviyyati, Adonai lee, v'lo ira*
> In God's hand I entrust my spirit, asleep as when awake,
> My spirit and my body too. God is with me, I shall not fear.
> Amen.

13 The Uncertainties of Life

One of the few areas of agreement by philosophers of all nations is the uncertainty of life. The Roman scholar Pliny the Elder said, "The only certainty is that nothing is certain." The Greek philosopher Heraclites drew a graphic image of life's ever changing condition: "You cannot step twice into the same river, for other waters are ever flowing unto you." The Roman poet Ovid wrote:

> There is nothing constant in the universe.
> All ebb and flow, and every shape that's born
> Bears in its womb the seeds of change.

Our own experience bears out the uncertainties of the human condition. Well today, sick tomorrow; rich now, but wiped out at the next stock market crash; a beautiful relationship may fall apart because of some misspoken words. You can take nothing for granted. Nobody can be absolutely sure about the next hour. Our security is ever shaken by unpredictable change—physical, economic, political—even natural catastrophes.

My sister in New Haven and I telephone one another each day. She has a stock answer to my "How are you?" She says, "Everything is under control!"

I always correct her. "Nothing is under control. You don't know what could happen from one moment to the next."

Of course, we make plans and manage to carry out many of them. But there is always an element of gambling in what we do, as Robert Burns indicated when he wrote, "The best laid schemes o' mice an' men/ Gang aft a-gley." (*To a Mouse*)

The Israel museum in Jerusalem has a display of Moroccan-Jewish wedding clothes. The bride and groom each wore a burial shroud under their festive clothes to be reminded of how quickly joy may turn to sorrow.

Nobody can be sure about anything in the immediate or long range future. A doctor in a small Polish town was known to first prescribe castor oil no matter what the illness. His patients, mostly ignorant peasants, never questioned this practice. When the town's teacher fell ill, the doctor also prescribed castor oil. The teacher asked, "Why do you prescribe castor oil for every ailment?"

"My good man," replied the doctor, "life is full of mysteries and uncertainties. We don't always know how to treat illness. But we know what castor oil will do and I want to start with a sure thing."

We all want a sure thing, but such does not exist. We can't be sure of anything. I saw a sign in Florida: "Life is short. Eat your dessert first."

What are the implications of life's uncertainties? If nothing is sure, so what? How does it affect your conduct of life?

When religious Jews talk about anything they plan to do in the future they add: "God willing" or "With God's help." It is the recognition of our dependence on circumstances beyond our control.

Your power, your freedom of will and action is limited. There is something tentative in everything you mean to do.

Frank Sinatra's theme song, *My Way*, boasted of his free will:

> I've lived a life that's full
> I traveled each and ev'ry highway
> And more, much more than this,
> I did it my way.

Not exactly. His way, as everyone's way, was largely shaped by others: family, friends, teachers, models—and by lucky or unlucky circumstances. The notion of the "self-made man" is fiction. Everyone is profoundly influenced by others, for better or worse. As Martin Buber taught: "all life is in relationships."

A realistic, honest self-image should induce a measure of humility. Avoid arrogance in over-reaching, in undertaking more than we can handle. In business, it is over-expansion. Ever so many enterprises have collapsed because of over-expansion.

In our private lives, we pay a heavy price for exceeding our limitations, getting involved in too many projects, accepting too many obligations, becoming excessively busy with social activities. The person who bites off more than he can chew over-estimates himself. He thinks he can do what he likes, forgetting that he is subject to events not of his choosing in this ever-changing life.

How should this fact influence your behavior and the way you deal with people? I suggest three responses to life's uncertainties.

First, heed the Latin proverb: *carpe diem*, meaning "grab the day" or "make the most of today." Yesterday is gone, tomorrow is non-existent. What matters is today. FOCUS ON TODAY. It's prudent to plan and prepare for the future. But that should not be your top priority. There may be no future for you. Therefore make the most of today. The Roman king-philosopher Marcus Aurelius, said: "We can live only in the present moment, in this brief now. All the rest of life is shrouded in uncertainty. Short is the life we lead....Confine yourself to the present."

The wisest of Frenchmen, Michel Montaigne, would free us of past regrets and future worries and focus on what you are doing at the moment: "When I dance, I dance; when I sleep, I sleep.... Rejoice in the things that are present; all else is beyond you."

Montaigne shared the mentality of the Chasidic master Moshe of Kobryn. When someone wanted to know what was most important to the rebbe, a disciple answered, "Whatever the rebbe happened to do at the moment."

Look at yourself. Isn't it marvelous that you are alive despite the countless hazards that may cut short your life? Somehow the destructive forces that assail your body day and night are kept in check or are overcome by a mysterious life-sustaining power. You may well share the sense of wonder of the psalmist who thanked God, saying, "I will give thanks to You for I am awesomely and wonderfully made." (Ps. 139.14)

What can fortify us against the uncertainties of life?

Perhaps the strongest support in daily life comes from friendship, companionship, and most profoundly, from a good marriage. "Two are better than one...for should they fall, one can raise up the other," so says our master teacher Kohelet in the Bible (Eccl. 4.9-10)

There is a price to be paid for friendship and, more so, for marriage. Care and attention to another person is a demanding but also a rewarding investment. Building friendship demands a steady escalation of contact and communication, from e-mail to telephone to face-to-face meetings. The old saying "out of sight, out of mind" may be platitudinous, but it is solid truth.

The Talmudic sage Yehoshua ben Perachya put it bluntly: "Buy a friend," (*Talmud*, Pirke Avot 1.6) meaning you don't get friendship for nothing. You must pay a price and make sacrifices for friendship and, certainly, for good family relations.

How to strengthen marriage calls for more than a lecture. The alignment of two lives, two personalities, each with his own needs, peculiarities, and idiosyncrasies, is the adult's greatest challenge.

What makes marriage different from all other relationships? It is the commitment to share and uphold one another in all the ups and downs of life. You can't expect that from any other relationship.

In view of life's uncertainties, I have so far stressed the wisdom of focusing on today and on all our present relationships.

I now want to mention a second response to life's uncertainties and that is: DON'T PUT OFF, don't delay what you want or need to do.

Our wise Hillel, who urged us to study a portion of Torah each day, added, "Don't say, I have no time now, I'll get around to it later; you may never find the time." (*Talmud*, Pirke Avot 2.5) I'd call that the anti-delay principle. I am as guilty as are you of procrastination. I keep under my desk a file marked "Unfinished Business." As time goes by, this file is filling up with jobs left undone. Edgar Guest lists some of these in his poem:

> Lord, So often we're postponing little matters near at hand
> Thou must fancy need for friendship men will never under-
> stand
> For some far-away tomorrow which we vision down the way.
> We keep putting off some kindness which we ought to do
> today.
> Week by week the list grows longer of the deeds we could
> have done;
> Letters promised to be written, that were never quite begun;
> Friends we meant to stop to visit and to do so set a date,

But death got there just before us, and we reached the door
   too late!
(*Regret*)

We all have lots of unfinished business: books abandoned in
the middle; the Bible we never got around to reading, a drawer
full of correspondence on which depends the life of a friendship
or precious relationship. These are not always broken; they often
die because we let them lapse. Our life is littered with good inten-
tions. Mind the poet's admonition:

I shall not pass this way again.
Through this toilsome world, alas
Once and only once I pass; if a kindness I may show
If a good deed I may do to a suffering fellowman
Let me do it while I can. No delay for it is plain
I shall not pass this way again.
(Quaker saying, attributed to Stephen Grellet)

Think also of your unfinished thoughts: beliefs hanging in
suspense between faith and doubt; a wonder in our soul, a great
perhaps, questions about God, about the meaning of life, its
purpose and death. Have you pursued these questions? Have you
looked into the answers Judaism might have? Is the development
of personal faith among your Unfinished Business?

One of America's most acclaimed artists was John Singer Sargent. He did the portrait of just about every important figure at
the turn of the century, including Presidents Theodore Roosevelt
and Woodrow Wilson. John Rockefeller paid a fortune for his portrait. Museums throughout the world show Sargent's portraits of
British and French noblemen, their attractive wives, and even children. But, of his own mother he made only one portrait, and that
he left unfinished. No doubt he was very busy; probably he said
to himself many times, "I'll finish mother's portrait just as soon as
possible. Obviously, he did not know nor heed Hillel's admonition:
"Say not, 'I'll get around it later.' You may never find the time."

My third response to life's uncertainties refers to the dark side of life, the losses we suffer as we age, our miscalculations and mistakes. The truth is that with each passing day, you win some and you lose some. I used to love skiing. But, at my age it's too risky a sport. It's a loss. But I have found compensation, the relaxing exercise of lap-swimming.

I can no longer give as much time to public functions and activities as in former years; instead, I spend more time studying and writing.

A Yiddish story wraps up one of the points I made about the uncertainties of life. A Jewish innkeeper in Poland went to see the landlord of the estate, a Polish aristocrat, to ask for the renewal of his lease. The landlord, who happened to be drunk, got into a rage: "I am doubling the rent next year." The innkeeper pleaded for mercy: "I can only pay the usual rent."

The landlord pulled a big dog on his leash and said, "Teach my dog to speak Polish and I'll let you stay with the old lease."

"How do you expect me to do it?" countered the innkeeper. "That's your business," said the landlord. "I give you one year's time. If you can't teach my dog to speak Polish, there will be no lease."

The innkeeper pleaded for more time. "Give me five years."

The landlord agreed and the innkeeper returned home with the dog. When he told his wife what had happened, she screamed, "You fool, why did you agree to such an impossible condition?"

He replied, "Silly woman, in five years much can happen. The landlord may die, or the dog will die or, God forbid, I may die. So, why worry about it now?"

The uncertainty of the human condition argues strongly for humility, for recognizing our limited control and knowing that the future is largely out of our hands.

Because we can barely see ahead one day at the time, don't delay, don't put off until tomorrow what needs to be and should be done. You are here today; tomorrow is doubtful.

The best way to live with uncertainty is to keep your eye on today and make the most of it. The Indian poet Kalidassa wrote 1,500 years ago:

Look to this day
For it is life, the very life of life
….For yesterday is but a dream
And tomorrow is only a vision
…Look well therefore to this day….
(*Look to this Day*)

14 Our Chronic Discontent

The first human pair, Adam and Eve, enjoyed the most perfect existence imaginable: No pain, no strenuous work, plenty of food, and all the amenities Paradise could offer. You would think that they should have been totally satisfied. But, as the Bible tells us, Paradise was not enough for them. They lusted for the one and only thing denied to them: the forbidden fruit. This they missed, and so, driven by their discontent, they lost Paradise.

Adam and Eve are symbolic of human nature. Discontent has remained a characteristic of the descendants of Adam and Eve to this very day. From the cradle to the grave, most people feel discontented for reasons, or for no reasons. This chronic discontent is the theme of Germany's greatest literary work, *Faust*, by Johann Wolfgang Goethe.

The aged Dr. Faust sadly realizes that none of the experiences of his long life have given him satisfaction. He reaches out to the devil with a deal: He will surrender his soul to him in return for a moment of contentment which he would wish to prolong.

Mephistopheles has Faust regain his youth and leads him through all kinds of experiences, but to no avail. He remains dissatisfied. Finally, in old age Faust undertakes the reclamation of land from the sea. Doing good to a large number of people brings him the contentment for which he had craved all his life. The drama of Faust underscores the place of discontent in life. We are not talking about the many trivial situations of justified dissatisfaction and complaints in daily life, such as dissatisfaction with a purchase or with the service in a restaurant or your attorney's handling of a case.

I am talking about the constant feeling that something is amiss; that things don't seem right; relentless worry, often not knowing why; unending fault-finding, a disgruntled mood and negative attitude toward life and a painful dissatisfaction with your own self and with your appearance and performance; feeling under-appreciated or insufficiently respected. The person having such feelings may not be diagnosed as depressed but as chronically discontented. What accounts for this sour mood about life?

The French philosopher Blaise Pascal suggested a surprising diagnosis of this condition: "All human evil comes from this—man's being unable to sit still in a room."

What did he mean? It is the drive for change, any change; the fallacy of the elsewhere; the notion that any change would be for the better; that elsewhere will be better than here, as the proverb says: The grass looks greener on the other side.

Rome's foremost poet, Horace, told his rich friends, "When you are in the city, you want to be in your country villa, and when you are in the country, you want to be in the city."

In other words, you can't sit still and be satisfied.

No doubt there are many who fantasize about changing their career, their location, even their spouse. This, too, may be the fallacy of the elsewhere. There is a Yiddish saying: "What one has, one does not want; and what one wants, one cannot get."

This kind of discontent is part of a persistent feeling that you are missing out on something. But as soon as you get what you want, you want something else.

Discontent is also related to faultfinding. Most families have at least one perpetual faultfinder. It is sad when it is a parent, a father or mother.

Dan Greenburg, In *How To Be a Jewish Mother*, tells about the mother who gives her son two ties for Hanukah. Being a good son and wanting to please his mother, he wears one to their next visit. She immediately notices and asks, "What's the matter, you didn't like the other one?"

Some of us carry a hurt throughout life because of a parent who was always critical of the way we dressed and ate and would not approve of anything we did and kept finding fault with us at every stage of life.

Some people must always have something to complain about. The story is told about a Mr. Finkelstein who was a patient at the Massachusetts General Hospital. Suddenly, without explanation, he checked out and transferred to a small, run-down hospital on New York's East side. There the registrar was curious why Mr. Finkelstein made the transfer:

"What was wrong with the Massachusetts General? It's an

excellent hospital."

"I could not complain about the hospital," answered Finkelstein

"Was it the nurses? Were they not attentive?"

"Oh, no, the nurses could not have been more considerate. I could not complain."

"So, was it the food?"

"The meals were tasty. I couldn't complain."

So tell me, Mr. Finkelstein, why did you move to our little hospital here?"

"Because here, I can complain."

When our patriarch Jacob was introduced to the Pharaoh of Egypt, the Pharaoh asked:" How old are you?" Jacob answered, "The years of my sojourning are 130. Few and evil have been the days of my life." (Gen. 47.9)

Jacob's assessment of life was not far different from that of the philosopher Thomas Hobbes, who defined life as "solitary, poor, nasty, brutish, and short."

Emily Dickinson agreed though in less dramatic words:

I'm Nobody! Who are you?
Are you—Nobody—Too?
Then there's a pair of us!
Don't tell! They'd advertise—you know.
(*I'm Nobody! Who are you?*)

I want to share with you three views of life, going from a deeply pessimistic to a remarkably positive attitude toward the human lot.

Woody Allen was interviewed as he turned 70. He talked with the interviewing journalist about life, sex, work, death and his generally futile search for hope. Wrote David Segal of the Washington Post: "The world according to Woody is so bereft of meaning, so godless and absurd, that the only proper response is to curl up on a sofa and howl for your mammy." He quotes Woody: "It's very hard to keep your spirits up. You've got to keep selling yourself a bill of goods, and some people are better at lying to themselves than others. If you face reality too much, it kills you." Not the least of Woody's obsession is the thought of death. "My 70 years will be spent better than those of a beggar at the streets of Calcutta. But we'll wind up in the same place." Speaking of aging, he says, "It's a constant struggle to see that your body doesn't break down. You put more time into maintenance and it's boring. It's just an awful thing and in that context you've got to find an answer to the question: Why go on?"

In sharp contrast to Woody Allen's gloom in spite of his fame, riches, and good health, is another celebrity who is amazingly upbeat in spite of his grave disabilities, which have brought him to the brink of death. I am referring to Art Buchwald, who at the age of 80, with his poorly functioning kidneys and the amputation of his right leg, resided in a hospice in preparation for death. Nonetheless, Buchwald laughed it all off in a column, entitled *Goodbye, Leg*.

> In my case, the loss of a leg interfered with my walking and getting in and out of cars. I required assistance of other people to do the simplest things, such as getting out of bed, getting into bed, and sitting in a chair.

After having been equipped with an artificial leg, he was assigned a physical therapist. He wrote:

> They are experts in pain and their main idea is that if there is no pain, there is no progress. I called my therapist a former prison guard at Guantanamo Bay.
> Once I made up my mind to get the leg, I decided to sell advertising space on it The good side to losing my leg—can you believe there is a good side to it?—is that everybody is nice to me.
> People rush to accommodate me....I have choice seats at sporting events, and the most important thing of all, a handicapped parking permit. Yes I am spoiled rotten.... Goodbye, leg. I didn't need you as much as I thought.

Buchwald proved once more that what is decisive is not what

happens but your attitude toward the happening.

How do you cope with a persistently disgruntled mood? How can you gain contentment in life?

The super highway to contentment is gratitude.

In every situation you can find something for which to give thanks, like the elderly spinster who added to her daily grace before meals, "And dear God, thanks for letting me keep my two teeth and especially because they meet."

There is wisdom in one of the most popular Pesach songs, the *Dayyenu*, which means "it would have been enough." This song of 14 stanzas lists 14 stages in the liberation from Egyptian slavery, each of which would have been enough cause for thanksgiving. The first says, "If God had only led us out of Egypt, but had not punished the Egyptians, *Dayyenu*—it would have been enough." Similarly, each of the following 13 acts of redemption is acknowledged with *Dayyenu*, it's enough for thanks to God even if He had done nothing else.

The *Dayyenu* teaches us that you don't have to have it all. Be satisfied with a piece of what you want, say *Dayyenu*—"It is enough."

Many of us are very ambitious; we want to expand; we want more success and more wealth. But too much of anything can ruin you, financially or physically. Know your limit.

Know when to stop. Know when enough is enough and say *Dayyenu*.

The drive to get all you can get is dangerous. Be satisfied with less than the maximum.

The wisest of all statesmen, Solon of Athens, said: "Do nothing to excess."

If you cannot get everything you want, enjoy the good you do have. Think of Matthew Arnold's poem:

Is it so small a thing
To have enjoy'd the sun
To have lived light in the spring
To have loved, to have thought, to have done....
(*Hymn of Empedocles*)

Saying it in prose: If you can eat, sleep, walk, enjoy reasonably good health, love and be loved by someone, and be self-supporting, you have the basic conditions for well-being. Be grateful. Every moment of gratitude is a step closer to happiness.

A professor at the University of California, Sonja Lyubomirsky, in her research on increasing happiness, listed eleven Happiness Boosters, the first of which is *count your blessings*.

"Keep a gratitude journal," she advised, "and once a week list three to five things for which you are thankful....If you name a particular person who has been kind to you or influential in your life, don't wait to express your appreciation. Write him or her a letter now, or visit and thank the person." (Interview in *Reform Judaism* magazine, Winter, 2011)

The wife of the popular author Rabbi Joseph Telushkin introduced a gratitude ritual in her Shabbat observance. It is not a ceremony nor a prayer. She simply asks all around the table: "What good has happened to you this week?"

Even if it was a tough week, you could probably think of at least one pleasant experience.

The other day I stopped on a main road to let a car turn from a side street into my lane. The driver was surprised, then threw me a kiss. It was a pleasant moment of goodwill interaction.

If you try, you'll remember all kinds of good things that happened, even something as trivial as hearing a human being instead of a recorded message on your telephone call.

The most personal cause of our discontent has to do with our self-image. There are no statistics but I guess many, maybe most, people feel that they are under-achievers; they keep thinking of unfulfilled hopes and dreams, of undeveloped abilities and talents, of having fallen short of their potential.

There is a long list of celebrities who rose from unpromising starts and setbacks to spectacular success. Don't let a rejection or setback drive you to self-contempt.

Marilyn Monroe, after only one year under contract with Twentieth Century Fox, was dropped in 1947 because the production chief, Darryl Zanuck, thought she was unattractive.

Tom Cruise auditioned for a role on a TV program and was

turned down because the casting director said he wasn't handsome enough.

In everyone's life there are incidents of which one is ashamed. How could I have said this or done so? You cannot un-make what was done. All you can do is regret, resolve to do better, and forgive yourself.

In forgiving yourself, you recognize that you are not perfect, that you have faults. If I forget that, my wife Maxine is sure to remind me.

The next step is self-acceptance mixed with a bit of humility. There is an element of healing in self-acceptance.

You must not be too severe in self-judgment. *The Sayings of the Fathers* include the remarkable statement of Rabbi Simon: "Do not regard yourself wicked." (*Talmud*, Pirke Avot 2.18)

You must not lose your self-respect; don't ever believe that you are too far gone. If you have made mistakes and wrong decisions, don't say, "I am a loser." Remember, the way to make good decisions is to learn from bad ones.

Give yourself credit for self-improvement; the way is always open for self-renewal. That's what Yom Kippur is all about. Repentance opens the door to a change for the better; you can improve relationships; you can rise to a higher level.

Forgiving another person who offended you is difficult, but in doing so, you do yourself a favor. Let bygones be bygone. Listen to Walter de la Mare's lines:

Poor Jim Jay
Got stuck fast
In Yesterday.
(*Jim Jay*)

If you want peace of mind, you must forget the unpleasant and move on with your life.

What are the ways to contentment in life? I suggest to you five rules:

- First, feel gratitude for whatever is right in your life. Be grateful for a good spouse, a loyal friend, for physical well-being (that is, more or less of it), that you can walk, hear, see, and are self-supporting.

- Second, realize that you were not given any guarantees in life. The future is uncertain. So, make the most of today and be surprised by joy.

- Third, it is good to achieve and succeed. Hope to win, but you can't be a winner all the time. Everybody is a loser some time. Accept a loss. Don't blame others; don't blame yourself. If you lose, it's not the end of the world. You win some and you lose some. So is life.

- Fourth, lower your expectations and you will have fewer disappointments. Expect less from people and you will get along better.

- Fifth, change anything to improve your life but accept what you cannot change and make the best of it. Never cease hoping and working for what should be, but accept, at least for now, what is.

The deepest source of chronic discontent is inherent in the human condition. We are stuck in a no-win situation over which we have no control. In Rabbi Elazar ha-Kappara's blunt words: "You are born to die; you were not born by your own volition and you must die regardless of your will."

We are tossed into life for some unknown purpose and under terms not of our own choosing. Some are born talented and beautiful; others, inferior and unattractive; some into poverty and others into plenty; some are disabled and others healthy and strong. None of us was given any entitlements at birth.

Our sages did not give us sweet talk, with pie-in-the sky promises, but realistically pointed to terms of life over which we have no say. Our rabbis would not go as far as Thomas Hobbes, who called the life of man "solitary, poor, nasty, brutish, and short," but they would not deceive us with the notion that we were created for our happiness. On the contrary, the two foremost sages, the house of Hillel and the house of Shammai and their disciples, in a debate that lasted two and one-half years, agreed that it would be better not to be born in view of life's many troubles and pains.

Nevertheless, and this is an amazing paradox, despite our grim realism, Jews are an optimistic people. Our toast is *L'chayyim*—"to life!" Every Rosh Ha-shanah, we wish one another "to be inscribed in the book of life." Israel's national anthem is *Ha-tikvah*—"the hope."

Our vision of the future is messianic, the triumph of good over evil. It is a hope based not on reason but on faith, the faith expressed in the first chapter of the Bible that at each stage of creation, God called it good. What seems evil in our life according to man's judgment, may, in the higher perspective of God, be part of a larger good. The God of Israel is not only the Creator but also the Redeemer. We keep faith with God, minding the prophet Habakuk's words: "The righteous shall live by his faith." (Hab. 2.4)

15 The Quest for Serenity

Charles Dickens opened his *Tale of Two Cities,* referring to the up-heavals of the French Revolution, with a series of contradictions:

It was the best of times. It was the worst of times.
It was the age of wisdom. It was the age of foolishness.
It was the season of light. It was the season of darkness.
It was the spring of hope. It was the winter of despair.

Today, in the aftermath of two world wars, the Holocaust, more genocides and, now, global terrorism, we seem to be heading into an age of unrelieved darkness, a long winter of despair, and far out of sight is the age of wisdom, the season of light, and the spring of hope!

A New Yorker, walking down Broadway, saw a little boy crossing the street straight into the path of a car. The man snatched the boy to safety. Then, he snarled at the boy, "What's the matter, kid? Don't you want to grow up and have troubles?"

How do you keep going in such dark and menacing times? How do you face problems the individual feels helpless to deal with? Turning the question to the private domain, how do you cope with personal vexations for which you see no solutions?

What might be pathways to serenity and peace of mind in this pathological age? However, I feel I can share with you a few points which in my personal life have helped me retain a measure of serenity and peace of mind.

I recently took an Amtrak train to New York and boarded the very last car of the train and was surprised to see a sign on the door that read "QUIET CAR." I asked the conductor what it meant.

"No cell phones," he said, "and no loud conversation."

It was the most pleasant trip to New York.

One way to serenity is to pause for some quiet time in a quiet place. Give yourself a break. Get off the treadmill of activities, jobs, and tasks that crowd your daily agenda. Listen to Psalm 127:

You who eat the bread of toil, it is vain for you
to rise up early and sit up late. (Ps. 127.2)

What the psalmist is saying is, don't get obsessed with the things you do. Don't try too hard to achieve because the psalmist gives you a reason in the next sentence:

God gives to His beloved in sleep. (Ps. 127.2)

This calls for an explanation. Anne Morrow Lindbergh wrote beautifully about the pacifying effects of the sea:

One never knows what chance treasures these easy un-
conscious rollers may toss up, on the smooth white sand
of the conscious mind...

And on the beach, Mrs. Lindbergh tells us, you learn to wait for the gift from the sea:

Patience, patience, patience is what the sea teaches.
Patience and faith. One should lie empty, open, choiceless
as a beach—waiting for a gift from the sea.
(*Gift from the Sea*, pp. 10-11)

The idea expressed so well by Mrs. Lindbergh is that switching, at times, from activity to passivity is beneficial. Without your do-ing, even while you are asleep, things may turn your way. Some of the most important gains in life are not gotten by hot pursuit but fall into your lap if only you will sit still long enough to let it hap-pen.

Isaac Newton was at leisure in an orchard when he saw an apple fall from a tree. Why did the apple fall down? The question sparked his discovery of the law of gravitation, one of the great-est scientific breakthroughs. An hour of unhurried reflection may open your eyes to things you are otherwise too busy to notice. Racing breathlessly through a busy day puts blinders on you. You are so bent upon your agenda that you can't see open doors of opportunity. Do nothing for a while each day and you will be surprised by good ideas that will pop into your mind. God's gifts may come to you unawares. As the psalmist said, "God gives to His beloved in sleep."

Americans, more than any other people, acclaim hyperactivism and condemn non-activity. We prove our worth by *doing* things. We feel guilty when we don't do anything.

A visitor from China was taken by his host on a long subway ride in New York. Before they boarded the train, the Chinese man noticed on the parallel track another train going to the same destination. "Why do you have two trains going the same way?" asked the Chinese man. "We are taking the express train," explained his host, "the other is a local train. On our train, we'll save at least 15 minutes." As soon as they emerged from the station at their destination, the Chinese man sat down on a bench.

"Do you feel all right? " asked his friend. "Perfectly fine," answered the Chinese man, "I just want to enjoy the 15 minutes we saved on the express train."

Anne Morrow Lindbergh spoke of treasures to be found on the seashore. You will not need to go seeking; you'll find them simply by waiting. Have faith that there is a generous Source in the universe that gives freely if only you are ready to receive.

John Burroughs wrote a poem entitled *Waiting*:

Serene I fold my hands and wait.
Nor care for wind nor tide nor sea;
I rave no more 'gainst time or fate,
For lo, my own shall come to me.

Another step toward serenity is to rid yourself of the notion that you and you alone are in charge of your life. To begin with, it is factually mistaken, an illusion. If you re-think some of the most important events or turning points in your life, you'll see that many of these were neither intended nor planned by you but happened due to the action of others or due to events you did not plan.

Egocentrics pay a heavy price for their distorted self-image. If you think that you are in control, you will blame yourself for every setback since, you imagine, as William Ernest Henley declared in his poem, *Invictus:*

> I am the Master of my life
> I am the captain of my soul

Henley's exaggerated sense of self-determination was parodied by Keith Preston, who wrote:

> I am the captain of my soul
> I rule it with stern joy
> And yet I think I had more fun
> When I was just a cabin boy

The reality is that no one is in full control of his life. In various degrees we are all dependent or interdependent. We are shaped by forces other than our own far more than we realize. Consider again the calming influence of the ocean. You cannot force your will upon it. The ocean is simply too enormous, too powerful. You have to take it as is. You must submit to its rhythm, its rising tide and the receding flow of the ebb. There is no sense of shame or defeat when you acknowledge the invincible power of the sea and yield to it. You simply accept the inevitable, the necessity of it all. And this is one of the secrets of serenity: to accept what *must* be, as Reinhold Niebuhr said so well in his famous prayer:

> God give me the serenity to accept things which cannot be changed; Give me courage to change things that must be changed; And the wisdom to distinguish one from the other.

To accept things that cannot be changed is not a prescription for indifference or fatalism—it is realism, the acceptance of limitations, the acknowledgment that "I am not God."

The late Menachem Shneerson, known to Lubavitcher Hassidim as the *Rebbe,* once received a letter from a man suffering depression. The letter read: I would like the Rebbe's help. I wake up each morning, sad and anxious. I can't concentrate. I find it hard to pray. I observe the commandments but find no spiritual satisfaction. I go to the synagogue but I feel alone. I wonder what life is all about. I need help.

The Rebbe returned a brilliant reply without writing a single word. All he did was circle the first word of every sentence and send the letter back. The disciple understood. The Rebbe had correctly diagnosed the cause of his problems. The encircled word was "I."

The ego is the biggest obstacle to peace of mind.

Many of us are our own worst enemy by exaggerated expectations, not only of others but of ourselves. The perfectionist is not satisfied with "good enough." He wants to perform beyond capability. He torments himself and others with chronic discontent. Asked how much wealth it takes to satisfy a person, John Rockefeller Sr. said, "Just a little more."

Up to a certain point in youth, we flatter ourselves with the notion that we can do anything we want to do. Maturity teaches us to recognize limitations. One of these is that you can't solve all problems. A good example is the frustration of parents who try so hard to shape a child in their own image. The parent desperately wants the child to benefit from his experience and may be absolutely right in pushing the child in a certain direction, but is rebuffed.

I once counseled a parent who was in tears over the child's course of action. "What more can I do?" cried the parent. My advice was: Face the fact that you cannot shape the child's life. Accept the child as is and count on any good you have done, by precept or example, to grow like a seed that will, in time, bear fruit.

The 55th psalm tells of a person so distraught by his problems that he wants to run away: "Oh that I had wings like a bird. Then would I fly away and be at rest. " (Ps. 55.7)

But soon enough he realizes that escape is no option. He must live with his problem. Finally, it dawns upon him that he is not the only player in his life. Other forces, other factors, God Himself, may have a hand in shaping his destiny. So he says or some inner voice says to him: "Cast your burden upon God and He will sustain you." (Ps. 55.23)

Know when to quit. Leave a little to God. Let go and let God!

Does this mean, God will do your job or solve your problem? Not at all. The end of the sentence, *He will sustain you,* suggests that you will still have to act, but with God's help. God may enable you to gain new insight or provide other means with which to work out your problem. *Cast your burden upon God* means "you are not the only player in your life; don't carry the world on your shoulders." Reach out to God in prayer and reflection. No one knows how God in response will reach out to you, but unless you take time out to listen with your inner ear, you will not perceive God's guidance and help.

Many of us are tormented by regrets over past mistakes and missed opportunities, or we worry about future problems. I strongly urge you to focus on today, on the matter at hand, on the present moment. A meditator in Zen Buddhism was asked how, despite his many tasks, he managed to be so calm and collected. He answered, "When I stand, I stand; when I walk, I walk; when I sit, I sit; when I eat, I eat."

"But I do the same," interjected the inquirer, "what do you differently?"

"No," said the sage, "When you sit, you think of standing up and when you stand, you are already mentally running."

The idea is to live each day to the fullest. Concentrate on this moment, this place, this person you are with. Don't live in the past with its regrets and don't be pre-occupied with tomorrow and its anxieties.

There is one other pathway to serenity and peace of mind. It is thankfulness. It has been drummed into the head of every well-brought up person to acknowledge every gift, helping hand or favor with a note or some thank-you expression.

Do you realize how many benefits you enjoy without a word of gratitude on your part? Charles Lamb said: "I am disposed to say grace upon 20 other occasions in the course of the day besides my dinner. I want a form for setting out on a pleasant walk, for a moonlight ramble, for a friendly meeting, or a solved problem."

The Radziner Rebbe reminds us of another dimension of thanksgiving: "When we come out unscathed by an accident, we give thanks; why not thank God for every day which passes without mishap? One who is cured gives thanks for recovery—why not give thanks when in good health and spared illness?"

Think of this: Hardly a day passes on which you might have been injured or killed or ruined by some mistake luckily caught in time. Add to these known escapes from harm the unknown dangers which you avoid day and night.

A man complained to his friend. "I am miserable. I can't pay my bills. "Then," consoled the friend, " be grateful that you are not one of your creditors."

A wit once wrote:

From the day you are born till you ride in a hearse
Nothing happens that couldn't be worse.

Instead of lingering on what you have lost, be glad for what is left. We should learn this lesson from the pilgrims, who instituted the first Thanksgiving in America. What kind of year was it for those 102 brave men and women who stepped off the Mayflower in 1621? It was a terrible year of hunger, disease and struggle with Indians: 6 died in December, 8 in January, 17 in February, 13 in March, more later, including governor John Carver and his wife. In that first year there were never more than 6 or 7 well at any one time. They leveled the graves so that the Indians could not count their losses. Yet they instituted a thanksgiving celebration for whatever good remained after all their losses.

Many people suffer from a depressing sense of failure; they feel that they have not lived up to their potential and classify themselves as unsuccessful. They should think again with Psalm 128 in mind:

You are happy when you earn your daily bread and see your wife within your house like a fruitful vine, your children round your table like olive plants. So shall a man be blessed who reveres God.

The psalm reminds us what really matters: self-support; a roof over your head; food on the table and a decent family life—these are the blessings that count. The rest, such as wealth, glamour, and power, are the superfluities, the frills that do not necessarily make you happier.

Whenever you belittle yourself as "unsuccessful," remember a remark of Ivan Turgenev, Russia's greatest and most successful playwright and novelist next to Tolstoy and Dostoyevsky: "I would gladly give all my success and fame just for knowing that someone worries about me if I am late for dinner."

Possession, contentment, and appreciation are different things: To the magnate who boasted of his vast estate, a poet said: "The land is yours but the landscape is mine."

You are rich if you expand your sense of appreciation and multiply thanksgiving.

As long as we are alive we are at risk. There is no insurance against adversity, harm, and pain. But we can respond in ways that restore serenity and some peace of mind, the pathways of which are:

- A half-hour or more each day for quiet time to collect yourself, changing pace from activity to passivity. Do so with reflection on a psalm or prayers. Even more beneficial is keeping every seventh day as Shabbat—a full day of cessation from all productive activities. It teaches us not to exaggerate the importance of our work and yield control to God, the Creator to Whom we owe everything.

- The second pathway to serenity is ego-management, mindful that many of the important things in your life happen without your doing. You are not the only player in your life. "Cast your burden upon God. He will sustain you."

- The third pathway to serenity and peace of mind is not to wallow in regrets over yesterday nor to torment yourself with worries about tomorrow but to focus on today.

- Finally, enhance your enjoyment of life by way of thanksgiving. Thankfulness is the twin of happiness. Practice thanksgiving so that life becomes thanks-living.

In these days, when we are horrified by atrocities which make us despair of humanity, we should note every act, however small, that restores hope in human goodness.

The German Jewish scholar Nahum Glatzer escaped the Nazi hell in advanced age. He told of an incident which restored his faith in human beings. He was standing on a busy street corner in Chicago when a little girl, afraid to cross the street, took his hand and trustingly walked with him to the other side. Then she ran off to wherever she had to go. The little girl's trust broke the spell of Prof. Glatzer's deep suspicion of human beings whose viciousness he had experienced under the Nazis.

It was like that one human footprint in the sand which saved Robinson Crusoe from his despair of loneliness. All the negative evidence of many years that his island was uninhabited was overruled by one single footprint. So one simple act of kindness might overturn all the negative experiences we may have had with human nature. So let us be patient and trust that good will prevail.

16 The Serenity of Sabbath

President Jimmy Carter's somewhat sermonic post-Camp David address to the nation included a remarkable statement on a national malaise of the spirit.

This was not the first time that a president of the United States has referred to a national malaise. In 1964, when Lyndon Johnson and Barry Goldwater were chief contenders for the presidency, both men expressed amazement at a similar mood of despair and discontent for which they could not account.

On July 16, 1964, Barry Goldwater, in accepting the Republican nomination at the Cow Palace in San Francisco, referred to "a virtual despair among the many who look beyond material success to the inner meaning of their lives."

Twelve days later, Lyndon Johnson agreed that there was a spiritual crisis. Speaking to a group of educators on the White House lawn, he said, "The most prosperous, the best housed, the best fed, the best read, the most intelligent, and the most secure generation in our history, all history, is discontented."

When presidents turn philosophers or preachers, they usually deal with the problem only in a superficial way. It is not enough to say we have a problem or to describe the painful manifestations of the problem. There is need to understand the underlying causes and also propose ways of coping with the problem. If we look for some understanding and solutions, we must turn from the politicians to the Bible.

Why is the richest and most powerful nation on earth so beset with self-doubts, so dissatisfied and discontented?

Part of the answer is suggested by the biblical expression: "Man does not live by bread alone." (Dt. 8.3)

In making this statement, our teacher Moses referred to needs that cannot be satisfied merely by material means. Regardless of wealth and other material advantages, we experience discontent. I have in mind two abiding sources of human discontent:

Robert Browning's advice that "a man's reach should exceed his grasp" causes discontent when such ambitions cannot be satisfied.

I think it can be proven that our discontent grows actually bigger in the more abundant, wealthier society.

The most contented are the most primitive people. When opportunities are near zero, society achieves the closest approximation of equality between its citizens. They tend to accept with fatalism and without envy conditions of life which all feel powerless to change. But a progressive and advancing civilization stimulates a bigger appetite than it can satisfy.

I remember a discussion in an Israeli kibbutz, the subject of which was why so many young people at the kibbutz are disgruntled. A grandmother stood up and made the following statement:

"When we started this kibbutz, we lived in tents. We ate out of tin plates. We had only one blouse and a pair of shorts and, most of the time, we were sick with malaria. But every night we sang and danced and were happy. Now, we have lovely houses with little flower gardens in front. We have a swimming pool. We have a luxurious dining hall, recreation facilities, and a library, but our children and grandchildren are dissatisfied."

The fact is that when life is easier and many more things become attainable, it hurts all the more if you do not get all of it. We are all the more frustrated when, with wonderful opportunities opening up for everyone, we somehow do not receive the top honors, top achievements, or top earnings.

We are apt to resent the inequalities in a time of plenty much more than we resent the burdens all must share equally in times of poverty.

How should we cope with this deep-seated discontentment, inspired by rivalry and envy?

Judaism's redeeming response has been to project different values. Before we open the Ark, we recite the 24th psalm:

Who shall ascend the mountain of the Lord and who shall stand in His holy place?
He that has clean hands and a pure heart; who has not profaned God's name and has not sworn deceitfully. He shall receive a blessing from the Lord! (Ps. 24:3-5)

There are different kinds of success in life. There is material success. There is the success of achievement and advancement in a career. There is the success of power, influence, and fame. But there is also the success of good sleep, of a clear conscience, of being unworried and unafraid, of being honored and loved by friends and family.

The Jewish scale of values by which success is to be measured includes integrity of character, honesty, and the goodness of heart as the highest achievements in life.

A man who might be considered a loser, coming in last in the race for material success, might, in reality, be standing very high on the mountain of the Lord in terms of the qualities of his character and moral worth. He might be greatly rewarded by the love and friendship of those who have come to know the goodness of his heart. To win the love and respect of only one other person may be far more satisfying than wealth and power. On the other hand, many of the extremely wealthy would gladly part with their riches in exchange for greater love and respect.

All this is meant by the Biblical expression: "Man does not live by bread alone."

There is a second and deeper source of discontent, one which human beings can never overcome. It is rooted in man's mortality. It is related to our inability to grasp the meaning of a life that is subject to pain and extinction. As Prince Hamlet puts it in his soliloquy, we must "suffer the slings and arrows of outrageous fortune....the whips and scorns of time...to grunt and sweat under a weary life...." (*Hamlet*, III, i, 59-78)

All of us pass through times when we are harassed and tormented by all sorts of troubles for which we can find no meaning. We cannot gaze at the dark and gloomy side of life too long without experiencing great uneasiness and spiritual distress. We crave relief from the bitter reality we see either in our own lives or in the lives of people dear to us.

How does religion respond to this craving for relief?

Some religions satisfy man's need for comfort by turning his attention away from the reality of this world to the dream of a happier future existence beyond this life. The Jewish response has been neither a denial nor a rejection of this world's reality, but the lifting up, the elevation of vision to a point from which life is seen in a larger perspective. Judaism summons us to see with the eye of faith the known and unknown together, the material and the spiritual in mystic union: "I lift up mine eyes unto the mountains whence cometh my help." (Ps. 121.1)

As faith stretches our horizons, we see our own mortality as mere moments of transition in the eternal renewal of life. Our tiny individuality is expanded in the historical perspective which says there is a God, a purpose, an order. Our discontent at the brevity of our own existence is relieved by the awesome awareness of the endless continuity of life from the very first gleam of creation down to this moment.

One of the few philosopher-kings in history, the Emporer Marcus Aurelius, said, "Live as on a mountain."

What did he mean?

If you seek serenity, you must rise above the jostling crowd of the market place, above the turmoil of contending forces, and create a kind of mental distance between yourself and the urgencies and pressures of the moment.

Seeing life with some detachment from the immediate needs and problems of today bestows upon you an inner calm similar to the sense of peace you experience when you look over a vast landscape from the top of a mountain. You can't hear the shouting and the noises that fill the streets of the town below. Its houses seem like match boxes. Its highways, so turbulent with traffic when you 're down below, now hold slowly moving caravans of tiny ants and appear insignificant compared to the surrounding mountains.

The stoic philosopher Marcus Aurelius proposed, "Live as on a mountain" as a permanent posture, an escape from the mundane concerns of daily life. It suggests an attitude of resignation, a withdrawal from the world.

The Jewish way to serenity is not that of permanent alienation, but of temporary detachment from the turmoil of daily existence at regular intervals. 'Six days shalt thou labor but the seventh is the Sabbath."

Sabbath is designed as an elevation to those spiritual heights where we recover the long-range perspective as a kind of balancing act against our excessive involvement in daily affairs. Excessive busy-ness with our daily tasks gets us to the point where we can no longer see the forest for the trees.

For the sake of our sanity and serenity, we must step out of the firing line of competitive living. We must get out of our frantic push and pull routine and rise to a point from which we can see life as a whole and its meaning not just in terms of today's screaming headlines but in terms of the everlasting realities.

Man has many cravings. He hungers for material things but also for peace of mind and serenity of soul. The Biblical expression "Man does not live by bread alone" is one of those signposts pointing upward to man's connection with a greater power and a greater purpose.

Our faith can lift us above despair by stretching our horizon beyond momentary reality, pointing to a spiritual dimension where success is measured by values other than those of the market place. Again and again, when exhausted by the weekday agenda of this and that, we need to be reminded on the Sabbath of our higher purpose, of our connection with eternity, which gives meaning to our own human existence.

17 The Case for Hope

I must confess to misgivings about my topic, *The Case For Hope*. My problem is that I myself am largely pessimistic and am groping for glimmers of hope. I feel like Dorothy Parker, who would inscribe her tombstone with the words: "Wherever she went, including here, it was against her better judgment."

It is hard to be an optimist. The news on TV and in the papers is depressing. Much in the human condition justifies despair. Our lifetime is plagued by illness, pain, fear and worry. We are vulnerable to all kinds of suffering and face the absolute certainty of death. How can you be hopeful? Is there a basis for cheerfulness, for optimism? Is it reasonable to be hopeful? Albert Schweitzer, the saintly physician and religious thinker who built a clinic in the African jungle, said, "My knowledge is pessimistic, but my will and hoping are optimistic." It is amazing that despite all the knowledge of evil in this world, we cling to hope. What would justify optimism in view of life's dark realities?

All of us face instability. We can't be sure about anything and are constantly menaced by unforeseen troubles. Overnight, our welfare turns to disaster. Every moment can bring us disappointment, frustration, defeat and loss. Is there a bright side to human existence?

The Roman philosopher Cicero justified hope with his saying, "As long as there is life, there is hope." The very uncertainty which threatens our sense of security may also bring relief, help and hope. Things could happen for our good.

When troubles beset you, cling to the hope that tomorrow everything may be different. Even the next hour may change your situation. Any time a new factor may arise that will turn a minus into plus. There is comfort in the truth that nothing is permanent in life. When as a little boy I got hurt, my grandma had these comforting words: "By the time you get married, the hurt will be gone." No problem, no trouble lasts forever. You may count on change though it may take time. If you have time, you have the minimal basis for hope. As long as there is life, there is hope.

There is another potential ground for hope. Our life is shaped not only by what we do but by factors over which we have no control. Unforeseen things happen—some of which may be to your advantage.

What is the difference between hope and wishful thinking? If you search the pavement for money, it is wishful thinking. Past experience does not justify the expectation of finding money on the street. But hope is an act of faith based on previous experiences. The hope of the ill for recovery is an expectation warranted by many cases of cure and recovery. Knowing people who were healed encourages your own hope for healing. It is not wishful thinking.

The idealistic hope for human brotherhood and peace is not a dream but an expectation grounded in experience, however limited, of friendship, helpfulness, and love.

The hope for success in your profession or business is kindled by your own past achievements. When my parents fled Vienna after having been robbed of their prosperous business, they arrived in New York with only $10 in their pockets. They did not know the language, and they had no connections and no bank account.

My father's first job was running an elevator at a high-rise in Manhattan. My mother borrowed a shipment of aprons to sell on a stand downtown on Manhattan's East side. Still, they did not despair. They were sustained by the hope that as they had lost and recovered businesses a number of times in Vienna, so now in America, too, there would be ups and downs; but they would work and achieve. And they did. Not many years later they owned property in New York and they eventually retired comfortably.

An African proverb says, "Any fool can count the apples on a tree, but no one knows how many trees there are in an apple." Nobody knows the potential powers and abilities that are locked up inside a person.

The magic key that opens up your full potential is perseverance. Thomas Edison attributed his many inventions not to genius but to persistence in hard work. Once, we are told, he assigned a special problem to one of his assistants. After a number of weeks the young man came back to Edison, very discouraged: "I have made 500 experiments and nothing works."

"You are wrong, young man," said Edison. "You have found 500 ways that don't work; now go back to work until you find the way that does work." He did as told and solved the problem.

In Judaism, hope is an article of faith. It is the ardent faith of millions of our people in the Messiah. When human efforts can no longer protect us against the evils which threaten our existence, God will empower the Messiah to come to our rescue. Moreover, he will usher in an era of justice, peace, and plenty. One of the *Thirteen Principles*, the summary of Jewish beliefs by Maimonides, says, "I believe with perfect faith in the coming of the Messiah and, though he tarry, I will wait daily for his coming."

However, there is a heavy dose of realism in our messianic hope. It won't happen in the near future but in the end of days; that is, at the end of history.

Why believe in messianic salvation? It is another way of saying: God cares for His creatures. He has the saving power and the will to rescue mankind from destruction. Wars will end some day in the future and history will move toward a happy ending.

Undergirding the belief in the coming of the Messiah is the cardinal faith that God knows and cares for His creatures and especially for His people of Israel. God will send the Messiah to save us from destruction and lead us into an era freedom and prosperity. The mass of our people clung to belief in the coming of the Messiah through centuries of turbulence, wars, and persecution—until the Holocaust.

The slaughter of six million of our people shattered the hope for the saving power of Messiah. If Messiah did not come to rescue our people from the gas chambers of Auschwitz, whenever would he do his saving work?

Every believing and thinking Jew is still struggling to explain God's non-intervention, or the Messiah's absence when most desperately needed. I have my own answer to the excruciating question: where was God in the Holocaust? I was inspired by a sentence in the Book of Psalms:

The heavens are the heavens of God
But the earth has He given to the children of men. (Ps. 115.16)

God rules the cosmos, but we human beings are in charge of life on earth. We were put in control of the earth, to manage it for better or worse.

This sentence from the psalms reinforces the Bible's view of human destiny as stated in the first chapter of Genesis: After creating man and woman, God charged Adam and Eve, the first human couple to "be fruitful and multiply, and replenish the earth and control it." (Gen.1.28)

With control comes responsibility. God equipped us to manage nature and create the human society. We were given the freedom of will to conduct ourselves as we wish; we are free to develop good or bad human relations. We can create societies of justice and peace or of violence, wars and holocausts.

But you might well ask, did Jews have a part in creating the Holocaust? Why was our people so horribly victimized? What have we done to be singled out for such suffering? I would answer: the most obvious lesson of human history is our interdependence. The wrong-doing of any one nation affects the welfare of all others. We shall be safe and well-off, enjoying freedom and justice only when all other nations enjoy these conditions. Human destiny is interlocked.

This truth is a summons to improve every society and work with all peoples to make the world safe for universal freedom and justice. This task is also the mission of the Jewish people, the very reason for our existence, to be, in Isaiah's words, "a light unto the nations." (Is. 42.6)

God showed love and care for humanity by enlightening our minds and guiding us in the right way by revealing Torah to Israel, the people chosen by God to spread its wisdom among mankind. The prophet Micah reminds us, "It has been told you, O man, what is good and what God requires of you: only to do justly, love mercy, and walk humbly with your God." (Micah 6.8) When Abe Lincoln was asked to which religion he belonged, he replied that he would belong to any religion which is based on Micah's summary of faith: "to do justly, love mercy, and walk humbly with your God."

The gravely ill, when giving up hope, turn to the wall. They have no expectations, and turning away from hope, they say "no" to all future possibilities.

Never turn to the wall of hopelessness. Keep hope and expectations alive. Think of yourself as a beachcomber, never knowing what treasures the ocean might wash ashore. But you must be looking for them, or else you will find nothing and miss opportunities that might come your way. Henry David Thoreau summed it up when he said, "Only that day dawns to which we are awake." You see nothing if you shut your eyes in hopelessness. Attitude is the primary factor of success and failure, as Longfellow affirmed in his three lines:

Not in the clamor of a crowded street
Not in the shouts and plaudits of the throng
But in ourselves are triumph and defeat.
(*The Poets*)

What should be your attitude If your hope is obviously in vain and cannot and will not materialize? Suppose you missed an opportunity for something very desirable ? Or you realize that you cannot advance in your profession? Or you have suffered an irretrievable loss? Or you have made a mistake that can no longer be repaired? Or a close relationship has deteriorated to the breaking point and can no longer be restored? Or aging, you must cope with the loss of energy and can no longer engage in sports and activities and go on long walks like you used to do?

What if illness leaves you handicapped and your good health is gone? I have myself gone through some of these losses and am trying to accept the situation. A song from Johann Strauss's operetta *Die Fledermaushas* has helped me bear those losses: *Gluck-lich ist, were vergisst, was nicht mehr zu andern ist*—"Happy is he who forgets what can no more be changed." Accept your irreversible losses. Go on with life.

It was a man of common sense who wrote this rhyme:

If you think you are beaten, you are.
If you think, you dare not, you don't.

If you like to win but think you can't
It's almost a cinch you won't.
If you think you'll lose, you are lost.
Life's battle don't always go
To the stronger or faster man
But soon or late, the man who wins
Is the one who thinks he can.
(Walter D. Wintle)

There is a potential power which will bring you either fulfill-ment or frustration. G.T. Chesterton said, "It is a sin to assume that nothing is being done unless *we* are doing it." The fundamental fact of life is that, for better or worse, we are always subject to the unforeseen and unpredictable actions of others, some of which might deliver the very things you hope for. We are forever ex-posed to uncertainty.

I have a word of advice for the aging among us. As you grow older, you let go of a number of hopes. You are no longer anxious for success, you may not be interested in another romance, you are no longer eager to travel, and you may not care to move into a better home. Hopes are reduced to the three essentials: health, the companionship of a good spouse or close friends, and finan-cial security.

When your hopes are reduced, you can increase gratitude for everything that is good and helpful In your life, from the trivial to major benefits. Be grateful for a good night's sleep, for an enjoy-able meal, for the helpful clerk at the bank or post office, for a kind and encouraging telephone call, for a good book, for friend-ships, for any pleasure whatever.

Thanksgiving is a wonderful tonic, the best mood-changer, and a step toward happiness.

How can a person of hope meet the challenge of the pessimist? What can you say to the pessimist who predicts failure and calami-ties?

I have tried to make the case for hope. In my first point I elabo-rated on Cicero's saying, "As long as there is life, there is hope." This is another way of saying that time is a great healer. That is, if you give it time, if you will wait, some of your problems will vanish. You may find solutions if only you will wait long enough.

I am thinking of problem children. I know of cases in which parents endured the pain of putting up with a difficult, troublesome child and waited long enough to see the child develop remarkable talents and improve his relationships.

Problems in marriage cannot be treated with generalizations. Each case is different. But every case calls for patience. With time and helpful counseling many a couple may reach a new understanding and make a go of their marriage.

You must not be disheartened by a professional or business setback. Personally, after any setback, I console myself with the truth that you cannot be a winner all the time. In life, you always win some and lose some. You are as strong as your endurance and patience.

Another reason for hope is the fact that things happen not always of your own doing. What you may not be able to do for yourself, others might do for you. Unforeseen events may bring you fulfillment.

18 Counting Our Days With Wisdom

Psalm 90 teaches us one of the most important lessons we should learn about life and death: "So teach us to count our days that we get us a heart of wisdom." (Ps. 90.12)

Think of life not in years, but in days. Whatever your plans for the next month or next year, today is what counts. Today you are alive. Who knows what tomorrow will bring, let alone the weeks and months to come.

How do we count our life time? Usually, we say, "I am so and so many years old." But there is a more realistic way of counting.

When you start on a trip, let us say from Washington to New York, you'll see a mileage sign, such as "250 miles to New York." As you keep driving, toward your destination, the miles listed on signs become fewer and fewer. So should we count our years on life's journey.

As our age goes up, the number of years to go goes down. Our remaining time diminishes. It is sobering to count your age not by the years you already lived, but by those still to be expected. That's how the insurance actuary determines your age, by your life expectancy rather than your actual age.

This way of counting will make you think of what is important for the remainder of your life; it will make you re-think your priorities and consider how to put your remaining years to their best use and not waste precious time.

Jewish ethical writings warn us against the sin of *Bittul Ha-sman*, which means "waste of time." What is a waste of time?

Hours of idleness, doing nothing, is not necessarily a waste of time, We need to get off the treadmill of busy-ness. We need pauses of inactivity. We need to think and re-think our agenda. We need to reconsider the goals we are striving to reach, our tasks, so many of which are self-imposed. If we took time to think, we might discover that much of what we do is unimportant and not worth our time, and that is *Bittul Ha-sman*—a waste of time.

Some of our heartaches are *Bittul Ha-sman*, such as crying over spilled milk, regret over some missed opportunity. Instead of bemoaning the past, look forward to every new moment which may bring a new opportunity.

A more serious *Bittul Ha-sman* is harboring grudges for injuries suffered some time ago. Such smoldering resentments are unproductive, wasteful of our time. As we grow older, we should not only remember but also forget some of our painful experiences.

Most important is the avoidance of new conflicts. Youth is ambitious for success and victories. Part of the wisdom we learn with age is that you can't win them all. Life is a succession of winning and losing. If you must always have your way, if you must win in every situation, you are bound to run into conflict. Take to heart the example of father Abraham. When conflict broke out between his herdsmen and those of his kinsman Lot over certain pastures on which to graze their flocks, Abraham said to Lot, "Let there be no strife between you and me...let us separate...if you will go left, I shall go right, and if you go to the right, I shall go to the left." (Gen. 13.8-9)

Conflict avoidance may seem like yielding. But most often it is the decision to change directions, to go a different way.

Jewish wisdom suggests three rules to live by.

The first rule to live by is live In the here and now. You don't know if you will be alive next year, next month or even tomorrow. So, make the most of today. Today is what counts, as John Greenleaf Whittier would have us see:

No longer forward nor behind
I look in hope or fear,
But grateful, take the good I find,
The best of now and here.
(*My Psalm*)

The preacher Kohelet in the Bible said to enjoy. "Eat your bread in gladness, drink your wine in joy...be happy with a woman you love, wear good clothes and look your best." (Eccl. 9.7-9)

The same idea is summed up in the Latin motto *carpe diem*— make every day count. In this respect the Romans were blunt to the point of grossness. At many a banquet, a human skeleton was seated as *memento mori*—a reminder of death, urging you to snatch as much pleasure as possible while still alive.

I listened to Randy Pausch's *Last Lecture*, which he delivered at the Mellon Institute in Pittsburgh. Knowing that he had only three to six months to live, he said, "I'm dying and I am having fun and I'm going to keep having fun every day I have left."

Do not wait until dying; enjoy God's gift of life now and every day. Unlike religions which glorify self-denial, fasting, sleepless vigils, and other forms of suffering, Jewish teachings urge us to appreciate God's gift of life with all its pleasures in the here and now. Treasure all the positive ingredients of the good life—health, affluence, a loving family. Most of our ceremonies are celebrations. The Sabbath, a day of spirituality, is also a time of *oneg*, of physical enjoyment, of leisure and pleasure.

The second rule to live by in the light of our limited lifetime is Hillel's "If not now, when?" Don't put off, don't postpone the good you can do or the joy you can have today.

Why are so many addicted to procrastination? Is the reluctance to act due to fear of failure? Is it a misguided perfectionism? Being cautious, waiting for the right time?

Our medieval philosopher Bachya ibn Pekuda wrote, "It is part of caution not to be overly cautious."

The wise Kohelet in the Bible put it this way: "The farmer who keeps watching the wind will never sow; and he who observes the clouds will never reap." (Eccl. 11.4)

Every action is risky but so is inaction. It is foolish to wait too long for the fulfillment of your dream, be it a career move, a lifetime wish to travel, study a foreign language, or learning to play a musical instrument. Whatever it is, remember Hillel's challenge: "If not now, when?"

The third rule to live by in view of our mortality is a Biblical instruction that became an English idiom: "Set your house in order" (II Ki. 20.1), meaning "settle your affairs." This refers not only to financial transactions, securing assets for your estate, and paying off debts; it is also a challenge to review and repair personal relationships. Seek the peace of mind that comes with reconciliation. If you bear a grudge and the resentment of wounded pride, get rid of all that bitterness. The only way to do so is to forgive and forget. The Talmudic definition of a hero is one who has control over his evil impulses; and the hero of heroes is one who turns an enemy into a friend.

An important strategy of settling your affairs is to simplify your life. Cut down on excessive engagements, drop burdensome projects, withdraw from complicated deals, and resign or disengage from causes for which you have lost interest. Concentrate on what really matters to you. In other words, reset your priorities.

Each stage of life has its own priorities: In youth, it is self- development, growth of knowledge, and skills in preparation for a profession. For adulthood, it is choosing a spouse, raising a family, and building one's career. In the latter stages of life, it is putting the years that remain to their best possible use.

I suggested three rules: First, make each day count. Don't miss opportunities for enjoyment. Second, don't put off the realization of your life's deepest wishes. Third, settle your affairs, simplify your life, reset your priorities. Focus on what really matters at this stage of your life.

The great rabbinic sage Hafetz Chayyim once said, "Life is like a postcard. At first, you write in big letters with wide space between the words. But when you get to the end of the card, you find that space has run out and you have not yet gotten to the most important things you wanted to say."

Focus on what really matters while there is still time. Time is your greatest treasure. As the psalmist said, "Count your days," meaning spend your days with wisdom.

"Setting your house in order" also means fulfilling aspirations, reading the classics you wanted to read, learning the language you hoped to learn. The journalist I. F. Stone, after retirement in his 70's, took up the study of Greek to read Plato and Aristotle in the original.

Mature people, and more so those advanced in age, need to revisit some of those deep, ultimate questions they may have tackled and dropped in earlier years. Is there a purpose to our existence? Why life? Why death? How do I know there is God? What kind of relationship and communication can you have with God? Does God hear and answer prayers?

Being Jewish means to study Torah daily. Why? To re-think our faith and the obligations—the *mitzvoth* or commandments—that our ancestors perceived as God's demands. It is not too late to become a student of Torah, not too late even for learning Hebrew to pray with understanding. I would urge the resumption of an old Jewish custom as part of "setting one's house in order." I mean the writing of an ethical will summarizing lessons one has learned so as to pass these on to children and grandchildren for the conduct of their own lives.

Old or young, we should count our days and reflect on the lessons gained from experience. This is wisdom, gained with age, to share with others.

There are age limits to physical growth but not to intellectual, moral, and spiritual growth.

It took me a long time to understand and appreciate Robert Browning's famous poem, *Rabbi Ben Ezra*:

Grow old along with me!
The best is yet to be.
The last of life, for which the first was made....

Considering the aches and pains that come with age, how could Browning say of old age that the best is yet to be? Was he serious or ironic?

Rereading the full, very long poem, I found clues to his meaning in these lines:

Learn, nor account the pang...
How good to live and learn
Amend what flaws may lurk.

Browning expressed the supreme Jewish ideal, which is a life of learning for the purpose of amending "what flaws may lurk"; in other words, life Is a journey of self-improvement fulfilled in old age.

Could Browning's expectation "the best is yet to be" refer to another stage of existence, to something after life that will be superior to the life we have lived? Could this life be just one of many stages of existence, leading to some unimaginable culmination of being?

This takes us from knowledge to the realm of faith. For my part, I leave this question open but recite each night this Hebrew affirmation of trust:

In his hand I entrust my spirit
When I sleep and when I wake
And with my spirit, my body too,
God is with me, I do not fear. Amen.

19 Making the Most of the Rest of Your Life

Our son-in-law, Rabbi David Forman, died at the age of 65. He was a vibrant personality, a bold leader, and a mesmerizing speaker, witty and challenging in his idealism. Because of an incurable liver disease, he knew that he would not live long. The diagnosis prompted him to write his book *Over My Dead Body,* in which he wrestled with his beliefs. Does God care about us? Is God good?

David held on to belief in God but questioned His goodness and fairness: "God is not a good role-model," he wrote. This should not shock you because we Jews have always felt free to question God's management of the world and to challenge His way with man. In this spirit, I want to ask some questions:

God, You commanded us to love you. Your Torah tells us: "You shall love your God with all your heart, with all your soul, and with all your might." But, do You love us, too? Is it love when You give us life only for us to decay and die? What kind of cruel joke is this life You have created?

I imagine God answering: Do I owe you anything? Who are you to hold me to account? You don't know the first thing about being and non-being. You have no idea why there is something, anything, instead of nothing. If I told you, would you understand? You speck of dust, you little worm dare to question the way I run the world I made?

So far, God has not chosen to tell me why there must be death. I have no choice but accept the fact of the inescapable end.

A minister preached a sermon on death. "Everyone in this parish will die," he declared—at which one man broke into a smile. "Why are you smiling?" asked the person next to him. "Because I am not from this parish."

Unhappily, human destiny is nothing to smile at. We must face inescapable decline and death.

The motion picture mogul Louis B. Mayer was asked to make a large charitable donation. "You can't take it with you," said the solicitor. "If I can't take it with me," answered Mayer, "I won't go."

Protest as you wish, the clock keeps ticking, and go you must. What consolation is there in the hope for immortality? If only we knew what is immortal. Is it the spirit? The soul? What kind of continuity? Do we retain our identity?

Many suspect that the whole notion of immortality is wishful thinking, yet even skeptics cling to this belief. Mark Twain confessed, "I have never seen an atom of proof that there is a future life and yet I am strongly inclined to expect one."

Does instinct overrule our reason?

We speak of the gift of life. A gift it is not. It comes closest to being a task whose purpose we cannot fathom. Long or short, it is an unfinished story which from beginning to end is wrapped in mystery.

Death drives home our colossal ignorance. We can explain countless details about life on earth but have no answers for the big question: Why is there life? For what purpose do we exist? If death is an exit, could it be an entry into some other form of existence? That is the great perhaps. You and I must live with uncertainty.

Uncertainty is the human lot: Rich today, poor tomorrow; jubilant today, downcast tomorrow; the life of the party today, on the deathbed tomorrow. The most admired Jew of the 19th century was Sir Moses Montefiore. Related by marriage to the Rothchild family, Montefiore made seven strenuous journeys to Palestine and traveled throughout the world in defense of oppressed Jewish communities.

When residing on his estate at Ramsgate, he had his butler solemnly announce every hour: "Sir Moses Montefiore, another hour of your life has passed." Montefiore wished to be reminded that time was running out and he had better make the most of the rest of his life.

That goes for each of us. What could you, what should you do to make the most of your remaining years?

Kohelet in the Bible tells us, in view of the brevity of life, "Go eat your bread and drink your wine with joy...wear good clothes; take care of your body and enjoy life with the spouse you love and...whatever you can do, do it by all means." (Eccl. 9.7-10)

Yes, pleasure is a good thing. Our sages tell us that on the Day of Judgment, you will be rebuked for denying yourself any legitimate pleasure you might have enjoyed because we must not reject the good things God created.

I would add to Kohelet's "eat, drink, and be merry" three suggestions of my own:

- REVIEW YOUR PRIORITIES. Focus on what is really important to you. A poet of ancient Rome, Horace, had it right: "Why aim at so many things in our short life." Cut your agenda. Simplify your life. Be selective. In work or retirement, concentrate on what means the most to you.

  Realize that your relationship with people is a barometer of happiness. Be attentive to family and renew contact with those with whom you have been out of touch. Let friends know you are alive. To keep a friend, be a friend.

- REVISIT YOUR UNFINISHED BUSINESS. The older we get, the more of our plans and projects fall into the category of unfinished business—hopes and dreams which we are unwilling to surrender; schemes which are close to our hearts but cannot be quickly realized; all kinds of good ideas and ambitions that had to be set aside for the time being. It is never too late. Grandma Moses commenced her long deferred career as an artist at the age of 75 and painted 1,600 paintings before her death at age 101.

  Then, there is the unfinished business of our home life. People living under the same roof often drift apart. Almost imperceptibly, distances grow between husband and wife or between parents and children.

  Two persons may walk hand in hand, yet feel alone, living together but not sharing thoughts and feelings. To find again the way to the other person's heart is one of life's most important tasks.

- LIVE ONE DAY AT A TIME—MAKE TODAY THE MOST IMPORTANT DAY OF YOUR LIFE. In youth, we are future-oriented, We build castles in the sky. We spin hopes and plans for the future. At later stages of life, we should stress today and not worry about tomorrow. The best way to make the most of the rest of your life is to make today count. Psalm 90 begs God, "So teach us to count our days that we may get us a heart of wisdom."

With limited time at your disposal, it is wise to sort out what really matters, ignore trivia, and unclutter your life. Focus on your relationships, live in the here and now; today is the day that counts. Don't put off; don't procrastinate. Do what you can, now! Be grateful for whatever good you can find in each hour, for a good friend, an interesting conversation, a beautiful song, and a lovely day. We Jews recite a thanksgiving blessing over a mere crust of bread. Be grateful for every little thing, even for a good night's sleep.

20 Our Mortality

My professor of sermonics once gave a lecture on *Topics a Young Rabbi Should Avoid Preaching*. "It is not seemly for a young rabbi," he said, "to preach on *How to Face Death with Serenity* or *How to Grow Old Gracefully*."

At my point in life, having passed the age of 95, the topic of death is no longer off limits.

It is difficult to work up enthusiasm on the subject of death. Yet a mature person will want to come to terms with the inevitable. Avoidance is so deeply ingrained in us that if death ever crosses our mind, it is usually the death of someone else, not of ourselves, as, for example, when a pious elderly couple reflected on their future. Said the husband, "Sarah, you and I should live till 120, but if it is God's will that one of us should die first, I shall definitely move to Israel."

Shakespeare said, "The sense of death is most in apprehension." (*Measure for Measure*, III, i, 76) Worse than death is the fear of it.

An Englishman, wanting to make death less frightening to family and friends, had his tombstone inscribed: "Cheerio, see you soon." Hardly reassuring, I should think.

To get rid of the fear of death is on the agenda of every religion and many a philosopher. Plato said, "The whole life of the philosopher is a preparation for death." How can one prepare for dying without sinking into depression?

Familiarity dispels fear. A visit to the dying will do more for you than for the one on his deathbed. Volunteers for hospice care will confirm what I have often observed—dying is nearly always a painless passage into final sleep. The end is usually an easy gliding into another sphere of being. The last words of one of England's greatest surgeons, Dr. John Hunter, were: "If I had strength enough to hold a pen, I would write how easy and pleasant a thing it is to die."

Mastering the fear of death calls for the opposite of avoidance: awareness and reflection. A practicing Jew who prays and reads his Bible, especially the psalms, cannot but learn to face death without panic. Daily, upon awakening, I recite the traditional thanksgiving for the restoration of my life. My daily prayers at home speak of God as the Source of Life who ordains death and reminds me that life is not a gift but a loan, that the soul inhabiting my body will be taken and remain with God unto eternity. The psalms echo repeatedly the comforting line: "Though I walk through the valley of death, I will fear no evil, for Thou art with me."

Jewish wisdom suggests that consciousness of death might enrich our life. Perhaps the most prodigious achievement due to a sharp awareness of death was that of the novelist Anthony Burgess. After being diagnosed with brain tumor and given only one more year to live, Burgess, in a furious outburst of creative energy, poured out five novels in a single year, and best of all, the tumor disappeared.

If death is the final extinction, we must wonder, what is the point of it all? Is there any meaning to the life and death of those trillions of human beings who have been and shall be born to grow, decay, and die?

In T. S. Eliot's play *The Cocktail Party,* one of the characters, Edward, tells the psychiatrist, "I am obsessed by the thought of my own insignificance." Is life an absurdity? Or, does it have some higher meaning and purpose, even though we can neither know it nor prove it? Alfred Lord Tennyson speaks for me in his humble admission:

Behold, we know not anything.
I can but trust that good shall fall
At last—far off—at last, to all
And every winter change to spring.

So runs my dream: but what am I?
An infant crying in the night
An infant crying for the light:
And with no language but a cry.
(*In Memoriam,* LIV)

Tennyson's poem mirrors Psalm 131:

God, my heart is not haughty nor mine eyes lofty
I do not exert myself in things beyond me
Or in things too wonderful for me.
I have quieted my soul like a weaned child with his mother.
(Ps. 131:1-2)

Why life and why death are unanswerable questions. Unwilling to follow the cynic who sees no meaning in life and death, I share the trust that speaks out of two words from Psalm 27, verse 10: *Adonai ya-asfeni*—"God will pick me up." Or, as a poet put it:

The dead are not bereft
Whoever falls from God's right hand
Falls into his left.

21 The Certainty of Death

After 9/11, an unknown author circulated a poem wondering what if this were the last chance to say to a dear one, "I love you."

If I knew it would be the last time,
that I see you walk out the door,
I would give you a hug and kiss
and call you back once more

If I knew it would be the last time,
I could spare an extra minute
to stop and say "I love you,"
instead of assuming you would know I do...

There will always be another day
to say "I love you,"
And certainly there's another chance
to say our "Anything I can do?"

But just in case I might be wrong,
and today is all I get,
I like to say how much I love you
and hope we never forget:

Tomorrow is not promised to anyone
young or old alike
And today may be the last chance
you get to hold your loved one tight

Take time to say "I'm sorry,"
"Please forgive me," "Thank you," or "It's okay."
And if tomorrow never comes,
You'll have no regrets about today.

There are all kinds of losses in life, but death is a radically different kind of loss. We can make up other losses; objects can be replaced. But what we lose to death is irreplaceable. With heightened watchfulness, we can prevent losses, but not death. It is the one absolutely inescapable, inevitable, and irretrievable loss we must suffer.

Grief-stricken King David put an end to his wailing and mourning over the death of his infant son, saying, "I shall go to him, but he will not return to me." (II Sam. 12.23) And so we must say in our hearts that our dear ones will not return to us. We shall go to them.

There is something odd about thinking of one's own death. We either never think of it, or we think about it all the time.

Does death have any meaning? Is there a way of quieting the fear of it? Many panic at the thought of it, and then rage against that prospect. Dylan Thomas wrote:

Do not go gentle into that good night
Old age should burn and rave at close of day;
Rage, rage against the dying of the light.
(*Do Not Go Gentle Into That Good Night*)

Edna St. Vincent Millay protested with even greater fury against death:

Withstanding Death...
I shall treasure my breath, I shall linger on.

I shall bolt my door with a bolt and a cable;
I shall block my door with a bureau and a table;

With all my might my door shall be barred.
I shall put up a fight, I shall take it hard.

With his hand on my mouth he shall drag me forth,
Shrieking to the south and clutching at the north.
(*Moriturus*)

When our Hasidic master Simchah Bunam (d. 1827) lay on his

deathbed, he tried to calm his weeping family: "Why weep? All my life has been given me to prepare for dying."

Is it possible to intellectually and emotionally prepare for death so as to face it with a measure of serenity? Not by denial or mental avoidance; we must familiarize ourselves with the inevitable; get used to the idea.

You don't have to become obsessed with death, but you'll be on the right road if on occasion you talk about it aloud as you review, from time to time, your life insurance and your will, buy burial ground, and write out funeral instructions, even when there is no sign of an imminent demise.

The witty Jonathan Swift tried to calm the fear of death with a rational argument: "It is impossible that anything so natural, so necessary, and so universal as death should ever have been designed as an evil to mankind."

Objectively speaking, for mankind as a whole, I may agree that nature is unthinkable without death, but subjectively and emotionally such reasoning does not take the sting out of death. We could reconcile ourselves to the death of everyone else, but not our own death.

The French novelist Andre Gide found reassurance by questioning the finality of death. Obviously something is ending at death. But, covertly and unknown to us, death may also mark the beginning of something new: "It is one of life's laws that as soon as one door closes, another opens. But the tragedy is that we look at the closed door and disregard the open door."

What could Andre Gide have meant by the other door opening at death? Some other form of being? What, if anything, is there in the hereafter? Is it some kind of ongoing existence? Perhaps a different kind of being altogether? The trouble is that the idea is so vague, so unimaginable—and we have no proof of anything in the hereafter.

If you are looking for certainty, face the fact that there is no sure thing in our understanding of death and whatever existence may follow it. The mystery is impenetrable. As the origin and the why of life is beyond our understanding, so is the meaning and necessity of death. The intellectual road to the understanding of death is a dead end.

How about the emotional level in coping with the idea of death? Before we can condition ourselves for the acceptance of death, we must come to terms with our own aging, and I now speak from experience. Socrates said, "Life is a teacher in the art of relinquishing." Sooner or later, we must let go, first of some of our possessions, then of some part of ourselves: the decline of physical fitness and, one by one, the losses of some of our capacities; we must get used to unfavorable changes in appearance and health and, then, more and more, we must let go of dear ones.

How pathetic and futile is clinging to what must be released. Instead of staring with nostalgia at the door that is closed, pay attention to the new doors that may open up, new opportunities for living meaningfully at every stage of aging.

Shel Silverstein, in his lovely children's story *The Missing Piece*, tells about a big wheel, a champion runner ahead of all other wheels. One day, a bad thing happened. It hit a bump and lost a piece of itself. After that as the wheel kept rolling along it felt a bump at every turn. It grew tired and lay down in the grass. For the first time, it looked straight up and saw the white clouds against the blue sky and heard the songs of birds. "Oh, this is wonderful," said the broken wheel, "I never had these experiences before."

That wheel learned an important lesson, that you may gain even when you have lost, that you may add some new range of experience and appreciation to your life, even when you let go of a part of yourself. Only when you let go of what can no longer be retained will you open yourself for new experiences, new friendships, new learning, and new pleasure. The one frightening aspect of death most difficult to deal with is the fear of the ultimate severance from all you know in what seems to us the absolute loneliness of death. But are we really cut off from everything in death?

In Mitch Albom's luminous account of conversations with a dying man, *Tuesdays with Morrie*, Morrie gives his view of death by way of a parable: A little wave bobbing along in the ocean is having a great time until it notices the other waves crashing against the shore. "My God, how terrible;" the frightened wave cries out, "look what's going to happen to me!" Then along comes another wave and it says, "You don't understand. You are not a wave, you are part of the ocean."

As we all approach the other shore, we must say to ourselves: I am not a wave, I am not an isolated being. Dead or alive, I remain part of the infinite ocean of existence as are all those who have departed before me. We all remain connected under God in the world, which is forever.

22 Living With Death on Your Mind

Reactions to one's inescapable death differ from person to person and at various ages. Most young people do not imagine dying. Death happens to others, not themselves. I was for the first time made sharply aware of my own mortality when an insurance agent tried to sell me a life insurance policy. He said, "You want to take care of Maxine and children in the event of your death."

Then he looked at me and, as a final sales pitch, told me what my life expectancy was according to statistics.

The Viennese novelist Arthur Schnitzler wondered if there was anyone who does not, deep in his soul, think of his death.

Mark Twain, on the other hand, was casual about death, saying, "I had been dead for billions of years before I was born and had not suffered the slightest inconvenience from it."

This is easily said as long as one is healthy and feeling fine. But when one is gravely ill and death is a close possibility, one is not likely to be so glib about the end of life.

Elie Wiesel published a book about his feelings when facing open heart surgery. While being wheeled into the operating room, he confessed to fear and anxiety as he looked at his wife, Marion, and son, Elisha. Would he ever see them again? The finality of separation from beloved ones is the most painful thought about death.

Could thinking about death have a positive influence upon one's way of life? Could there be benefits that go with the fear of death? I suggest three possible benefits:

The first is the cooling of ambitions, the lessening of passion in the pursuit of success as you realize that whatever you could gain, you can't take it with you. Thinking about one's death will make success and failure less important. In fact you realize that most things we fret about are not important. You don't have to be #1 in any enterprise to enjoy life. That is a step toward serenity.

My second suggestion is not to torment yourself with idle speculations about death. Just make the most of the days you are alive. Kohelet, whom our sages called *he-chacham,* the wise man, summed it up in a few words: "eat, drink, and enjoy." (Eccl. 3.13) Attend all happy events of family and friends; don't postpone your own celebrations;

don't put off things you enjoy doing. You live only once.

Carl Sandburg wisely said, "live not in your yesterdays, not just for tomorrow, but in the here and now." Our rabbinic sage Hillel made the point 2,000 years ago: "If not now, when?"

My third suggestion, in view of the inevitable expectation of death, is to take to heart the two-word sentence in the Book of Psalms, repeated three times in Psalm 37. It is the admonition *al titchar*— "fret not." Suppress anger and resentment as quickly as possible; don't keep blaming yourself or others for mistakes; don't brood over failures and disappointments; no one is perfect; forget and forgive injuries; don't try to change people, including your spouse and children; accept what is and limit expectations.

We think of our own inevitable demise.

We know it must happen, sooner or later. Some are obsessed by the thought of death. Others try to suppress it. Sigmund Freud struggled so hard to avoid the confrontation with death that he would not even attend the funeral of his 95-year-old mother. Yet try as we may, there is no way of keeping death out of mind. A fallen leaf or a dead bird could trigger thoughts of our mortality.

At times we wonder what it is like to die? If only we could ask any of our departed, how was it? What happened? Where are you now?

We ask Omar Khayam's question:

Strange, is it not? That of the myriads who
Before us passed the door of Darkness through,
Not one returns to tell us of the Road,
Which to discover we must travel too.
(*The Rubayyat,* XLIX)

In that charming children's book, *Letters to God,* one little kid writes:

Dear God: What is it like when you die? Nobody will tell me. I just want to know. I don't want to do it. —Your friend, Mike

William Blake, on his deathbed, told his wife, Catherine, that dying was no more than moving from one room to another.

Dietrich Bonhoeffer, when taken to his execution, said to the two Nazi guards who evidently were sorry to take part in ending his life, "For you it is an end, for me a beginning."

This was an answer of faith, not knowledge. None of our sciences, none of our philosophies can tell us what, if anything, remains after death besides dust and ashes. The sum total of human knowledge does not cover even a trillionth of the cosmic reality into which we are tossed to flicker with life for a split moment. Whatever death may be, it is not the end of our being. We are not getting out of this world in death. We are being transformed into another state of being. But in whatever form, even as pure spirit or soul, we do not fly off into another world. We remain in this world.

The Hebrew term for the hereafter is revealing: *Olam Ha-ba* means "the world to come." It is this world, only at a later point in time, not another world. The synonym "departure" for death is misleading. We go nowhere but remain in this world forever connected with all there is; whatever remains of us after death, remains under God's will and care, as Psalm 91 puts it: *b'tsel shaddai yitlonan*—"You abide in the shadow of the Almighty." (Ps. 91.1)

Is there any meaning to the life and death of those trillions who have been and shall be?

Leon Tolstoy's *The Death of Ivan Ilych* tells of a respected civil servant who, in his final illness, is not haunted by the fear of death but by the feeling that his life was wasted. Remembering and reevaluating the various stages of his career, he sees nothing worthwhile in his life. After childhood and education came a series of disenchantments: disappointments in marriage and in his career. He says, "I had been going downhill while I imagined I was going up."

He recognizes an inner emptiness: "I was going up in public opinion but, to the same extent, life was ebbing away from me. And now it is all done and there is only death?"

So, he wonders, what is the meaning of life? Why? It can't be that life is so senseless. The thought suddenly occurs to him:

"Maybe I did not live the way I ought to have done?...What if my whole life has been wrong?....Was it all a waste?"

What is tragic about Ivan Ilych is that he did not take stock of his life until he was near death. He waited to reflect and to evaluate his life until it was too late to change it. What a pity if a person keeps on trotting out his days like on a treadmill, not going where he really wants to go, not accomplishing or doing anything satisfying. The time to assess, reconsider, and possibly re-direct one's life is while one is well and able to change course.

An hour or merely a half-hour of daily undisturbed reflection, best in the morning, might clear your head and help you get a better hold of yourself and prompt you to change what needs to be changed. That is one of the benefits an observant Jew gets from his daily morning prayers.

Death on your mind could enhance your life if it prompts you to do the following three things:

- DON'T PUT OFF WHAT IS IMPORTANT TO YOU. We all make plans and resolutions and then bury them through procrastination. James Albery wrote:

  He lived a life of going-to-do
  And died with nothing done.

  Whenever you postpone any good plan, project, or action, even as small a matter as a visit or letter you owe someone, tell yourself Hillel's wise words: *Im lo ach-skav, ematai?*—"If not now, when?"

- DON T WEAR YOURSELF OUT WITH FEARS ABOUT THE FUTURE. Live one day at a time. At my age, one hour at a time. If you concentrate on doing well what should be done today, the future will take care of itself.

- LIVE WITH UNCERTAINTY. You cannot be sure of anything. Be amazed that you wake up alive in the morning and be thankful at night for having gone through the day. Trust that your life has some purpose or meaning even if you will never know it. What meaning there is to our existence is known only to God. Our Maker must know why we were made. You are not alone, in life and in death.

23 You Are Not Alone

One of the most famous poems of the 20th century is entitled *Lullaby for Miriam.* The author, Richard Beer-Hofmann, a Viennese Jew, tells of thoughts that crossed his mind as he put his baby daughter to sleep. It is late afternoon and the sun is setting:

> Sleep, my child, sleep.
> Look at the sun, the sun is dying
> Sinking behind the mountains in shrouds of red.
> What do you know of the sun and death?

Somberly he reflects on the child's destiny. If only he could give her his life's experience. In vain parents try to do that.

> Blindly we go and we go alone,
> No one can anyone's partner be

He realizes, she'll have to live her own life. But he wonders, is any person the sole possessor of his life? Is our existence something entirely separate and isolated? Is anyone really alone in this world?

> We are but riverbeds. Through you and me
> Runs the blood of the past to those who shall be,
> They are all in us, Who is alone?
> You are their life—their life is your own

Thus the poem speaks of the human condition with its opposites of birth and death, of solitary, individual existence and the bond that binds generation to generation.

Lullaby for Miriam was published all by itself as a single page book. Rainer Maria Rilke, the century's greatest poet, memorized it, and on his trip to Sweden, aristocratic families would send their carriages for him so that he might recite the poem for them.

What explains the profound appeal of this poem? It is the allusion to man's fate of loneliness and death, redeemed by the greater reality of the unity of life, our link with all the generations that have ever been. A sharp awareness of loneliness is not limited single persons, the widowed and the elderly living alone.

An anonymous poet wrote:

There is a mystery in human hearts
And though we be encircled by a host
Of those who love us well and are beloved,
To everyone of us, from time to time,
There comes a sense of utter loneliness.

Even in the midst of a crowd, or when happily married and surrounded by family, we may experience a poignant pang of loneliness, a loneliness of the heart, a sense of not being understood. A crucial part of yourself cannot be communicated. No matter how close, how intimate you are with another person, there remains a gap that cannot be bridged. There are things about you no other person will ever know. Adrienne Rich says so in her lines:

Two strangers, thrust for life upon a rock
May have at last the perfect hour of talk
That language aches for; still—
Two minds, two messages.
(*A Marriage in the Sixties*)

We think of our families, the living and those no longer alive. Our thoughts turn to our departed. They say "time is a great healer," but there are sorrows that cannot fade away. My son-in-law, Rabbi David Forman, wrote a very personal article for the *Jerusalem Post* about his sister's death when, at age 12, she was run over by a streetcar in Boston. He did not actually know her because the accident happened before he was born.

He was told only that she was an angelic child. David writes that when his father at age 91 made his last trip to Israel, "he went to the wall...and found a seat adjacent to it, and motioned to me to sit next to him. His voice trembling, he said, 'There is not an hour in the day that I do not think of her. I stand before these stones imploring God to return her to me.' There is nothing more painful than the death of a child."

138

When a parent dies, we lose a large measure of our past; when a child dies, we lose a portion of our future.

There are limits of understanding between persons. Most people don't even understand their own deeper selves. We must be grateful for whatever was and is good in our relationships and not look for the perfection which is beyond human reach.

A man was eagerly looking for a spouse. Friends introduced him to suitable ladies but he found fault with every one of them. Finally, he found the one he thought was the perfect woman—but there was no match because she was looking for the perfect man. The best relationship does not seek perfection but tolerates imperfection.

My sister and I, as children, would occasionally get into an argument. I would try all my methods of persuasion to change her mind, often to no avail. She just wouldn't budge, and if pressed for an explanation, she'd cut me off with the infuriating answer, "You'll never understand." I have come to see that there are indeed things about each of us no other person will ever understand, simply because, as Adrienne Rich put it, "Two minds, two messages."

There will never be total disclosure and understanding between two persons. As Emerson wrote in his diary, "We never touch but at points." One can be with people and yet be lonely. Loneliness is not being alone but feeling unrelated; that is, not communicating. This is the point of Jean Ingelow's poem:

Man dwells apart, though not alone,
He walks among his peers unread;
The best of thoughts which he hath known,
For lack of listeners, are not said.
(*Afternoon at a Parsonage*)

In Lewis Carroll's fantasies is an incident of a padlock with arms and legs that says to everyone it meets, "I'm looking for a key to unlock myself." Many of us are locked up in ourselves. We have a sense of futility. What is our purpose? What our reason for existence? We go through life looking for the key to unlock life. And we don't find it because we keep looking for it in ourselves. We should be looking beyond ourselves. The meaning of our life is in relationships, in connection with something greater than ourselves. The meaning of our personal, individual existence is embedded in the totality of life—ultimately with the Maker of life. It is God Who has the master key to each of us. Think of the psalmist's words: "Lord, Thou hast been our dwelling place in all generations." (Ps. 90.1)

God is the ground of our being. "Before the mountains were brought forth, Or ever the earth and the world were formed, Even from everlasting to everlasting, Thou art God." (Ps. 90.2)

It is God Who calls within our souls: "Return, ye children of men." (Ps. 90.3)

Acknowledge that you are part of the original context of life from which you were torn for the short time of your existence and to which you are destined to return.

In the light of faith, loneliness is an illusion. No being is ever cut off from the totality of life. As Richard Beer Hofmann said, "They are all in us. Who is alone?"

The medieval philosopher Master Eckhart expressed our paradoxical sense of existence as separate beings, yet forever connected with the totality of life and with its Maker:

That I am a man
I have in common with all men.
That I see and hear
And eat and drink
I share with all animals.
But that I am I is exclusively mine,
And belongs to me
And nobody else,
To no other man
Nor to an angel nor to God
Except in as much as I am one with Him.

This is the mystery of the Shema: God is one, the world is one, life is one, even the living and the dead are one.

You are not alone. You are forever connected with God, the Creator with Whom are the spirits of all flesh.

24 Death Is Not the End

The Biblical sage Kohelet made a statement which at first sight, sounds absurd. He said, "It is better to go to the house of mourning than to the house of feasting: for that is the end of every man and a living person should take it to heart." (Eccl. 7.2) Feasting at a party is certainly more enjoyable than sharing the sorrow of mourners, but the company of mourners will be more helpful. It will help you face your own mortality and the death of dear ones.

What is there about death that Kohelet would have us take to heart? When the Russian-Jewish novelist Isaac Babel was dragged away by Stalin's KGB, he was heard to shout, "But I have not been given time to finish." One of the great truths about life is that life has no finish. It is without beginning and without end. Much of what we want to do in our own lifetime remains unfinished: Many a life tells of passionate relationships which somehow faded; soaring ambitions which vanished; projects that had to be abandoned and hopes discarded.

Jewish wisdom recognizes our incapacities yet adds a challenge: Rabbi Tarfon in *The Sayings of the Fathers* (*Talmud*, Pirke Avot 2.21) said: *Lo alecha ha-melachah ligmor, v'lo ata ben chorin l'hibatel mimmenna.*—"You are not bound to complete the task, but neither must you disengage yourself from it altogether." In other words, do what you should as best you can. You may not be able to solve a family problem, meet a financial need, or resolve an issue of relationship, but you must help to the extent you can.

A former editor of TIME magazine, Charles C. Wertenbaker, was told that he had terminal cancer and only one more year to live. In a moving chronicle of that final year, his wife records that from that moment on, the two most often spoken words in their home were "important" and "unimportant." Consider the things you fret and worry about. You'll find that many if not most of those things don't matter one way or the other.

Death consciousness is the broom that sweeps pettiness out of your life. "Life is too short to be little," said Benjamin D'Israeli.

What you learn in the house of mourning with its sharp awareness of death is a new scale of priorities, a new perspective on values. Averell Harriman was an undistinguished rich playboy until his sister, Mary Rumsey, died in a riding accident. She had been a social worker with a strong social conscience. It was reported that her death motivated him to go into public service. He excelled as a statesman and diplomat, the chief negotiator of the nuclear test ban treaty, serving the cause of peace in memory of his sister. Confrontation with death in the house of mourning brought out the best in him.

What do we fear about death? Is it pain? Having witnessed the dying of many persons, I have observed not agonies but relief from pain. Physicians tell me that death itself is painless.

Do we fear the unknown? Or, the final severance, being cut off from everything, the fear of extinction?

Our Hassidic master, Nachman of Bratzlav, had some profound thoughts about the connectedness of all things. The universe is multi-dimensional. This life is something transitional, a short phase, moving across a narrow bridge toward another dimension of being.

The point is that in death as in life we remain connected with something greater than ourselves. We, creatures of flesh and blood, do not last long in our physical condition, but whatever connects us with God is eternal.

25 A Ray of Light from the Kaddish Prayer

A legend tells us that God sent one of His angels to mingle among humankind and bring back the most precious thing he could find. The angel returned with a tiny little bottle. God asked, "What makes this so precious?" The angel replied, "I saw a man sobbing with regret over something he should have done or failed to do, and I caught some of his tears in this bottle." God approved of the tears of regret as something most precious.

Tears of regret wash away whatever poisons our relationship; they cleanse us of guilt and help us form a new self-image and a new bond, even with those who have gone from this life.

Is death the ultimate separation, or will our death be the portal of reunion with those who went before us?

Most people, the young more than the old, choose ways of denial. Death is something that happens only to others. But all must come to terms with the unalterable fact that the human mortality rate is 100 percent.

Can we make the certainty of our mortality more acceptable? What could help us tolerate the prospect of death?

Reform Judaism's standard prayer book, *The Gates of Prayer,* includes reflections on death prior to the mourner's Kaddish. These are meant to comfort the grief-stricken.

With reluctance I share with you my personal aversion to these reflections. I find no comfort in them. Consider the opening sentence of one of these meditations: "The contemplation of death should plant within the soul elevation and peace."

On the contrary! The parent who is shattered by the death of a child, the grief-stricken spouse or the person thinking about his own death, feels anything but an elevation of soul and peace. The contemplation of death, which most of us try to avoid with a passion, gives us discomfort mixed with anger, not elevation of soul and peace.

An alternate meditation draws a graphic analogy of life with a flickering candle: "Life is finite," we are told, "like a candle, it burns, then It fades, and it is no more...yet we do not despair."

Wrong again! Of course, we do despair. The death of one we love and thoughts about our own death push us to the brink of despair. Smug and pretty words do not express our anguish.

The Bible reflects much more accurately the mentality of people facing up to death: With a mixture of hurt and anger, the psalmist challenges God: "What profit is there in my blood when I go down to the pit? Shall the dust praise you? Shall it declare your truth?" (Ps. 30.10)

The psalmist could not rationally justify death. Neither can we. Why go through life with all its experiences, pleasures, and pains? Why accumulate knowledge, even wisdom, only to vanish in oblivion? Is the Creator a sadist, making us vulnerable to all kinds of suffering before blowing out that flickering candle we call life?

If we wonder why death, we should also ask, why life? What is its meaning? For what purpose has life emerged in the universe? A bereaved mourner, humbled by ignorance of why life and why death, put up a tombstone for his beloved wife and had it inscribed:

Here lies Jane Shore
I say no more.

I am tempted to stop at this point and say no more but feel I should share with you at least some rays of light I find in our tradition.

Do you know what the Kaddish prayer is saying? Isn't it strange that the Kaddish, recited by mourners, has not a single word about death? Listen to the translation:

Magnified and sanctified be the great Name in the world which He created according to His will. May He rule His kingdom in your lifetime and during your days and in the life of the household of Israel, soon and speedily. May His great Name be blessed forever and ever.

Blessed, praised, glorified, exalted, elevated, adored and lifted up for praise be the Name of the Holy One; blessed be He, beyond any blessing and song, praise and consolation that uttered in the world. May there be abundant peace from Heaven and life, upon us and upon all Israel.

What, in plain words, is the Kaddish saying to the mourner and to all of us who crave a vision beyond death? The clue is the lavish outpouring of praise for God in the Kaddish. What it says is, you who are weeping over the passing of life, know that there is One Who is more than life and you are connected with the One Whom we praise above all things in this world.

26 Jewish Wisdom for Conducting Your Life

While serving as director of the Hillel Foundation at the University of Buffalo many years ago, I heard of a curious litigation. A student sued the University for a refund of his tuition fee, claiming that he had been misled by a statement in the University's catalogue. It said that liberal arts students would gain wisdom through their studies. Standing before the judge, after his graduation, he argued, "I request the refund of my tuition fee because I don't believe I am wise."

The Judge passed sentence with these words: "Knowing that you are not wise is proof that you have indeed gained wisdom. Case dismissed."

Actually, we do some self-judgment every day, consciously or subconsciously. At various times, each takes a measure of himself, evaluates his life or some aspect of it, however superficially or in depth. You ask yourself: What do I want? Am I getting there? Do I meet my expectations as a person, spouse, parent?

It's an easy guess what most of us want: health, security, getting on with people, some respect, and to be loved by someone. These are the components of success and happiness.

Can Judaism help you realize these wishes?

I invite you to consider three insights by Jewish sages: first, what to aim for in life; second, what to avoid; and third, how to reduce stress.

What to aim for in life

As for your aim in life, you want to feel good about yourself and be well off. Ben Zoma, a second century sage, hit the nail on its head with his saying, "Who is rich? *Ha-sameach b'chelko*—Whoever is pleased or contented with his portion."

Contentment is a unique treasure. With contentment, you have everything. Without it, you have nothing. Psalm 131 says, "I do not go after things too big or extraordinary for me." (Ps. 131.1)

I pity those who do not know when enough is enough, who do not know their limits, who can't stop striving. When J. P. Morgan was asked what he wanted in life, he answered with a single word:

"MORE!"

By contrast, I want to mention a Jewish mathematical genius, Gregory Perelman. This 43-year-old bachelor who lives with his mother in Russia was awarded the one million dollar Millennium Prize by the Clay Mathematics Institute of Cambridge, Massachusetts. Though unemployed for four years, he said he's got to think about whether to accept the prize. He learned to live without the things riches can buy and prefers a life in quiet obscurity.

Another way to contentment is to avoid comparing yourself with others who are more successful, more handsome, more athletic, more popular, and richer than you. Accept what you are, what you have, and what you can do.

Don't indulge the fallacy of the elsewhere, thinking the grass is greener on the other side. Think twice before wanting any change, imagining a change would be a change for the better. It might be worse.

Advertising agencies appeal to the mania for change. I recently received an advertisement by the Tempur-Pedic Mattress company, a photo of a bed with new mattresses, and the caption: "Give us 7 minutes. We'll change your life."

Before making any change in your life, try to appreciate the good in your present situation.

Practice the habit of thanksgiving. Observant Jews pepper their conversation with *Baruch ha-shem*—"God be blessed." How are you? *Baruch ha-shem!* Did you sleep well? *Baruch ha-shem!* How is your wife? *Baruch ha-Shem!* Accentuate the positive. Count the things that are okay and be grateful.

Ben Zoma's point is that wealth should be measured not by how much you have but how much you appreciate what is already yours. You are rich if you can find contentment with yourself, your spouse, your family, your friends, your work, and your health; and if not in good health, be grateful for those physical abilities you still have.

Thanksgiving paves the way to contentment. "Happiness," wrote the novelist John O'Hara, "is only for greeting cards. Contentment is what we have to achieve."

Having said all that, I recognize a downside to contentment. It could degenerate into lethargy or indifference to suffering and evil.

I have many reasons for personal contentment but am deeply dissatisfied with the social ills of poverty, domestic violence, the high crime rate, terrorism, and the ever-present danger of another war.

In view of these facts, discontent is not a bad thing. It is the engine for improvement. It drives ambition; the New Jersey based Borden Dairy Company, boasting of its superior dairy products, chose the slogan "Our Cows Are Not Contented "

What if you are beset by problems, illness, debts, poor income, troubling family relations, and setbacks in business or professional career? Under such circumstances, how can you even talk of contentment?

Nothing in life is permanent. If at one time you achieve contentment, it may be short-lived and be gone the next day, even the next hour. In that case, discontent is natural and inescapable. But then, remember: The causes for discontent are likewise changeable. King Solomon, the wise, whenever he was happy or sad, glanced at a ring on his finger. The ring was inscribed with the words: *gam seh ya-avor*—"This too shall pass."

So how do you overcome discontentment? If things are bad, be grateful that things are not worse. Even in the worst of situations, you might see something, however small, that is good and be grateful for it. Gratitude is the world's best mood changer. And remember Solomon's ring: Everything changes and a change for the better is always possible. Be patient.

What to avoid

From contentment which is not always achievable, Jewish wisdom turns to something to be avoided at all times.

Rabbi Eliezer, a first century sage, said: *al t'hi noach lich'os*— "Do not quickly burst into anger." (*Talmud*, Pirke Avot 2.15)

This rule is reinforced in many passages of the Bible and Rabbinic literature: The 34th psalm warns us that anger will cut short your life: "If you want to live long and enjoy life, guard your tongue from evil." (Ps. 34.13-14) According to a Harvard study (2004), some 30,000 heart attacks are triggered each year by outbursts of anger.

The Book of Proverbs cautions us: "Do not befriend an angry man lest you learn his way." (Pr. 22.24-25)

The Talmud suggests a three-fold character test: *bchisso, b'chasso, b'chosso*—how you handle money, anger, and drinking. (*Talmud*, Eruv. 63b)

There is enough stupidity and evil around to make you angry every day. How can you get the upper hand and curb your anger?

Anger management is not easy, as acknowledged by the Book of Proverbs: "He that is slow to anger is superior to the mighty and he that controls his spirit is stronger than the conqueror of a city." (Pr. 16.32) Sometimes it is more effective to respond with wit than with anger: When Lady Astor, notorious for her poison tongue, told Winston Churchill, "If I were married to you, I'd put poison in your coffee," Churchill replied, "If you were my wife, I'd drink it."

An article in the *New York Times Magazine* (Aug. 15, 2010) recommended exercise as a means of working off anger. The exercise I suggest is an exercise of the mouth.

If you are tempted to make an offensive remark, remember Sam Levenson' s counsel how to be wise: "Just think of something stupid to say, and then don't say it."

What can you do—short of therapy—to control your anger?

Thomas Jefferson' s method for keeping his temper in check was to count to ten, and if necessary, repeat counting, before responding to infuriating words or deeds.

One of our rabbis in Poland needed more time to cool off. So, when provoked, he would run upstairs, change clothes and return calmer and in control of his temper. The idea is to cool it; to take time out before you react to an annoyance or irritation.

The psychologist Pauline Wallin, author of *Taming Your Inner Brat,* advises special caution with e-mail. She suggests to wait up to an hour before dashing off an angry message. When letters were written the old way, it took a while to finish and more time to re-read, with a good chance that you might cool off and, on second thought, tear up the letter and never send it.

With e-mail, the moment you finish the message, you are likely to click the "send" button. Think twice before clicking the "send" button. My advice is to leave a nasty message as a draft and re-read it an hour later before you decide to send it.

One thing to avoid when angry is to rehash a list of previous offenses, the recall of which only escalates anger. This often happens in marital quarrels when both sides treat one another to a history of their respective faults.

If there is still enough reasoning power left while bursting with anger, see the issue in proportion. How important is the cause of your irritation? In all probability, the frustration, indignity, or inconvenience which aroused you at the moment will seem trivial and unimportant a few days later. Benjamin Franklin gives excellent marital counsel with his statement: "Before marriage, keep both eyes wide open; afterwards, keep them half-shut." For the sake of harmonious marital relations, practice the art of overlooking, of ignoring issues of lesser importance.

So, stop and think before you speak or act in anger. The best advice ever given on anger reduction is in the Book of Proverbs: "A gentle answer turns away anger." (Pr. 15.1)

Jewish wisdom provides one other strategy against anger. Yehoshua ben Perachya said, "Judge everyone on the scale of merit." (*Talmud*, Pirke Avot 1.6) Don't be hasty to judge a person by one unpleasant incident. If you knew that person better, you might find some good in him. The humorist Will Rogers said, "I never met a man I didn't like." You may not match such generosity of spirit, but if you look carefully, you are likely to find some redeeming quality in the person who made you angry.

How to reduce stress

The pharmaceutical industry rakes in billions with remedies for worry, stress, and tension. The most normal person will at times be stressed out. You cannot avoid tension at work and at home. People have different ways of coping, from taking a deep breath, to drinking, to jogging.

Is there a preferred remedy in the Jewish wisdom tradition? I personally have found two words in Psalm 37 helpful: *al titchar*— "don't fret." (Ps. 37.1,7,8) These two words, urged upon us three times in the same psalm, mean literally "don't get hot," that is, with worry, anxiety, or resentment.

How can you prevent it? The answer of Psalm 37 is "tum your

situation over to God." (Ps. 37.5)

Psalm 55 puts the same thought more forcefully: "Throw your burden on God." (Ps. 55.23) Unburden yourself, disengage yourself from the problem that weighs so heavily upon you.

But how can you take your mind off a major worry at work, a worry in the family, or a serious illness?

Moreover, what if you are skeptical about God's intervention on your behalf? What if you can't think of God as a rescue squad who will, on demand, solve your problem?

Let us, for the moment, leave God out of it and start not with faith but fact: realize that you are not the only player in your life. Countless unforeseeable factors shape your destiny. These forces, other than your own, are not all necessarily bad; among them may be undreamed of solutions to your problem—call them accidental or benevolent acts of God.

My point is: Don't imagine that everything depends on what are doing. Don't try to carry the world on your shoulders. You may not even be the chief actor in the drama of your own life.

It is amazing, even heart-breaking, how many of us don't recognize our limits. We sometimes waste ourselves on impossible tasks. Typical is the case of Franz Kafka and his father. Kafka had the all-consuming aspiration to be a writer. His father, an industrialist, wanted Franz, his only son, to take over the factory. The attempt to change the son's self-image and life vision was futile and only produced conflict.

If you are not satisfied with a major personality trait of your son, daughter, or spouse, don't delude yourself with the notion that you can turn him or her into a different person. You must accept him or her as is, even as he or she must accept you as you are. Acceptance is the heart of contentment. Accept the limits of what you can do with your life and how much less is your power to shape the life of another person.

Jewish wisdom touches on all aspects of life. We dealt with only three topics:

The first is how to achieve contentment, the chief ingredient of happiness. It is closely linked to appreciation. The author of Psalm 128 wanted to draw a scene of happiness. He did not set it in a palace with gorgeous interior, surrounded by beautiful gardens. The setting he chose was a humble home of domestic tranquility: Parents at peace with one another, at a table with their children. "You are happy and truly blessed," says the psalm, "if you support yourself and are at home with your wife and children."

Contentment does not require riches, glamour, and fame. Gratitude is the twin of contentment. It is yours if you appreciate what you have, what you do, and what you are. Be thankful not only for what is good in your life but for what remains after life's inevitable setbacks and losses. "My rheumatism is very bad," said the long suffering patient, "but, thank Heavens, I still have the arm to have it in."

The second topic we developed is anger-management. When problems, frustration, and resentment explode into anger, remember, anger will only make things worse. Moreover, anger is self-destructive. "You will not be punished for your anger, but by your anger," said Buddha, and then he illustrated the point: "Holding on to anger is like grasping a live coal intending to throw it at someone else; meanwhile, you are the one who gets burned." Jewish wisdom agrees and strongly advocates anger control.

The third counsel of Jewish wisdom is the practice of self-limitations. When under pressure and worried, it is wise to unburden yourself. You are not the only player in your life. You are not in total control of your life. Set limits on your responsibilities and expectations:

That man is blest
Who does his best
And leaves the rest;
Then do not worry.
(Charles F. Deems)

Those who are believers will count on powers other than their own and place themselves into the hands of God. So shift your burden upon God; in short, let go and let God.

27 The Case for Prayer

William Buckley once said, "A sure way of not being invited again to a dinner party in Manhattan is to talk about God."

I take the risk and talk about God because without belief in God, every synagogue, Yom Kippur, and all other services are irrelevant. Seeing our people crowding the synagogue on Yom Kippur raises the question: why are they absent on the regular Shabbat? Why do only two to three percent of liberal Jews return to their pews on the average Shabbat? What was it that made our great grandparents flock to the synagogue daily—many even three times daily—and worship at home, reciting blessings for all kinds of daily functions? They needed no synagogue, journal, or website to remind them of services; they did not have to be attracted to the synagogue by gimmicks, special events, concerts, entertainment, and sensational guest speakers. *Interest* was not a factor. Interested or not, they came to worship, motivated by faith and a sense of mandate. They did not come to be inspired or turned on; they came to pray, not looking to be filled with new faith but bringing their own deeply felt faith, and they were eager to express it. What faith? That there is a God Who hears and answers prayer. Were there doubters among the mass of Jewish believers? Certainly, but they were few and worshipped anyway, doubting their own doubts,

The majority of Western Jews today no longer share the faith of our fathers. Ours is a generation defective in faith, riddled by skepticism. The God, affirmed by hundreds of generations with the Shema Yisrael exclamation, has become a question mark.

It is little comfort to us that Christendom has suffered a still greater decline in membership and Church attendance. The fact is that every religion has taken a beating in the Western world during last 300 years. The enlightenment of the 18th century abrogated the divine authority of royal government, toppling monarchy after monarchy; then it challenged traditional morality and religion. Next came Charles Darwin's theory of evolution, which contradicted the Biblical account of creation; then the philosopher Ludwig Feuerbach, who declared the God idea to be nothing but a projection of human qualities, a mirror image of human nature—in other words, a figment of the imagination. Sigmund Freud reinforced this denial of God's existence with his theory of God as a magnified father image, an infantilism to be outgrown by mature people.

Most destructive of faith has been the horror of two world wars, the Holocaust, and a seemingly unending chain of new genocides. How can one maintain faith in a benevolent, all powerful God Who rewards good and punishes evil? Who hears and answers our cries for help?

Modern artists of the theater of the absurd express the spiritual despair and emptiness of the human condition. The playwright Samuel Becket was walking with a friend through a London park. It was a beautiful day. The friend, exuding great joy, said, "Becket, on a day like this, isn't it good to be alive? Becket muttered, "I wouldn't go that far."

Your mood about being alive much depends on your beliefs or doubts. Is there any meaning to human existence? Does a higher order or Intelligence operate in our life and history? Do events just happen, or do they happen justly? Do events happen at random or do they follow a moral order? Can we derive a sense of security from a God who watches the scene and does something about it?

The biologist Ernst Haeckel, one of the leading scientists of modern times, said that if God allowed him to ask a single question, he would ask, "Is the universe friendly?" In other words, what evidence is there that God knows and cares about human needs and suffering? What about the immense suffering in our world? Innocent children are wasting away with all sorts of diseases, and adults are brutalized, raped, and massacred.

Where is He when we need Him? Before I try to confront our doubts, I want to give skeptics and atheists their due.

Alexander Dumas expressed his outrage in these words: "If God were suddenly condemned to live the life He has inflicted upon men, He would kill himself."

His compatriot, Stendhal, declared, "The only excuse for God is that He doesn't exist."

Woody Allen said, "I don't think God is evil, but basically He is an Underachiever."

Friedrich Nietzsche minced no words in announcing God's obituary:

"God is dead!"

How can a believing Jew respond to this atheistic assault? What do we know about God?

Prof. Arnold Eisen, chancellor of the Jewish Theological Seminary in New York, was asked to discuss God in 300 words or less, At first he thought this limitation was absurd but then he realized that 3000 or even 300,000 words wouldn't do. The problem is not a limitation of words but man's limited mental capacity.

A child was digging a hole in the sand by the seashore. "Tell me kid," said a man, "what are you digging for?"

"I'm making a hole to pour the ocean into it," said the child.

Equally childish and futile is the attempt to get God, the Supreme Being and Source of the Universe, into that tiny web of tissues we call the human brain.

One of the leading Jewish thinkers of our time, Rabbi Louis Jacobs of England, favored this prayer:

Lord, give us the grace
To teach the whole race
We know nothing whatever about Thee.

Pascal, a profound believer, said, "It is incomprehensible that God should exist, and it is incomprehensible that He should not exist." No rational argument can clinch the case for God. Faith in God is not gained by logical evidence or knowledge but by hunches, intimations, and intuitions, and most of all, by the example of persons of faith.

Believers do not know God like an object that could be understood and described. Walt Whitman wrote:

I say to mankind
Be not curious about God
For I, who am curious about each,
Am not curious about God....
I hear and behold God in every object
Yet understand God not in the least.
(*Song of Myself*, v. 48, 1855)

I once conducted a wedding at which Tommy Corcoran, trusted advisor of President Roosevelt, was asked to give a toast to the bride and groom. He raised his glass and said, "To the bride, may you always try to understand your husband and love him. To the groom, may you always love your bride, but don't try to understand her."

We may have a sense of God's presence, we may somehow feel connected and relate to God; we may love God. But trying to understand God is futile.

The foremost modern Jewish thinker, Martin Buber, was asked by his friend, Pastor William Hechler, chaplain of the British Embassy in Vienna, the following: "Tell me, do you believe in God?" Buber was caught short by the question and said something reassuring without really answering the question. Only later it occurred to him what he should have said: "If you want me to speak of God in the third person, what He is and how He acts, I'll have to say, no, I don't believe in a describable God. God is real for me only when I address Him as You. God can be addressed but not expressed."

Addressing God, reaching out for God's help, looking for God's presence—all this is wrapped up in prayer. However, for many, prayer is a problem. Can a person learn to pray with conviction? What could make prayer a satisfactory experience? Many of the 150 psalms overflow with joyful enthusiasm. The anonymous authors, probably lay people, share with us their prayer experiences; while they pray, some break into song and dance.

No doubt, there are pleasurable aspects of the worship experience—the social fellowship, the music, the singing, the mood conducive to reflection. But all these are trivial compared to the real purpose of prayer. What is that purpose? It is making contact with God.

This calls for a certain mindset. What if you are not in the mood? What if you lack conviction that there is a God who hears and answers prayer? What if you feel like you are praying to a wall? Should you mumble words without conviction?

The prophet Amos said, "Prepare to meet your God." What kind of preparation?

The Hasidic Rabbi of Tzantz recognized serious obstacles to meaningful prayer. He said, "Before I pray, I pray that I may be able to pray."

Speaking for myself, I admit I am not always ready to pray. What conditions, what feelings, what thoughts make me want to pray? High on my list of motivating, even compelling, reasons for prayer is a sense of powerlessness, of vulnerability. We all live on borrowed time. Our existence is precarious. Suddenly our strength is gone. None can be sure to make it to the end of the day.

How often have you answered a question about your well-being with a response like, "Everything is under control." Do you realize that "everything is under control" is a blatant untruth?

The truth is that nothing is under our control. Nobody controls his own body, let alone his fate or destiny. We are all subject to instant extinction. This is the basic human condition which drives me to prayer. "Man's extremity is God's opportunity." In our weakness, we turn to the Almighty for help.

Abraham Joshua Heschel defined prayer as "an invitation to God to intervene in our lives." But will He? I do not pray with any certainty of an answer but out of necessity, in view of my need. I have no idea what happens to my prayer once I have offered it up to God. Yes, I wonder each time if my prayerful petition will be granted.

The moment I apply reason to prayer, I am beset by doubts. I imagine the case of a woman who prays for God's help to conceive a child. Is it thinkable that the Creator of the universe, with its trillions of constellations and countless creatures, will intervene in the biological-sexual process of this one woman?

Was William James right in saying, "Religion is a monumental chapter in the history of human egotism."

The idea that God is on call, ever ready to intervene in our lives, can lead to frivolous demands on God. A movement sprung up a while ago called "Pray at the Pump." People would encircle gas stations, hold hands, and plead for divine intervention to lower gas prices. This is on the mental level of the 6-year-old girl who wrote, "Dear God, thank you for my baby brother, but what I prayed for was a puppy."

What about serious prayers, such as recovery from illness, rescue from peril, or guidance in a critical decision?

Such prayers raise a question: How important are we that God should bother about our welfare? With billions of worlds whirling about space and unimaginable multitudes of living beings in the world, why should God reach down to any one of us to pull us out of the mud? Why would our paltry needs merit the attention of the supreme power of the cosmos? Human logic cannot make the case for God's intervention in our lives.

Yet our inability to understand a thing is no proof that it cannot be. If something is inconceivable, that does not make it impossible.

Tennyson, who shuttled back and forth between faith and skepticism, would not give up on prayer. He wrote: "More things are wrought by prayer than this world dreams of," and then he wrote:

> Speak to Him, thou, for He hears
> and Spirit with Spirit can meet
> Closer is He than breathing,
> and nearer than hands and feet.
> (*The Higher Pantheism*)

For me the most troubling question is God's non-intervention in those catastrophic disasters as earthquakes or tsunamis, whose innocent victims are in the hundreds of thousands. If God, the Creator of nature, is loving, all knowing and all-powerful, why won't He intervene to save us?

Try to think through what God would have to do to save us from natural disasters. It would require no less than the suspension of the laws of nature. At God's command, flood waters would have to freeze, or run backward into the ocean, or evaporate into the air. Under such conditions, millions of fish and sea-animals would perish. Since that did not happen, I am forced to conclude that much as human life may matter to God, it must be more important to let the forces of nature run their course. In other words, God has bigger irons in the fire than the salvation of every human being.

Still, most Americans and many doctors believe that God can intervene to save dying patients. The *Archives of Surgery* reports that "57 percent of adults said that God's intervention could save family members even if doctors declared that treatment would be futile.... Nearly 20 percent of doctors and other medical workers said that God could reverse a hopeless outcome." ("Trauma Death: Views of the Public and Trauma Professionals on Death and Dying From Injuries," Aug. 18, 2008)

Think what you will, the ways of God are inscrutable. Isaiah got it right when he warned against applying human standards of thinking to God: "'My thoughts are not your thoughts, neither are your ways My ways,' says God" (Is. 55.8)

It is fruitless to speculate just how our prayers move God. All we can talk about are the fringe benefits of prayer within ourselves. Every time we turn to God in prayer, we also turn inward and gain insight into ourselves. We sort out feelings, anxieties, and needs, and we examine our consciences.

If your prayer is not answered, persist. The value of persistent prayer is not that God will hear us, but that we will finally hear Him. Above all, prayer gives me the feeling of a connection with God. If prayer gives you nothing but a sense of God's presence—that is no small gain. Twelfth century Spanish Jewish poet Judah Halevy made that point:

Longing I sought Thy presence;
Lord, with my whole heart did I call and pray
And going out to meet Thee
I found Thee coming to me on the way.

How can you meet God? How could you experience God's presence or closeness? Countless people have moments of illumination with a sense of God's presence. Those experiences are unpredictable. Suddenly one is struck by the certainty of being with God. Others have that experience at the sight of the roaring sea or the immensity of the starry sky. And many are just amazed at being alive and feel connected with God.

I do not propose bizarre ways of mystic seclusion, breathing exercises or the recitation of some mantra. Personally, I get a sense of connection with God when reading the Bible, especially the Book of Psalms. Many of the 150 psalms are spiritual autobiographies of ordinary people. Far from naive, some psalmists were highly sophisticated people that questioned God's failure to respond to prayer.

"Why are you silent?" they complained. "Why are you hiding?"

Read the psalms with pen and notepad; jot down any sentence or phrase that speaks to you and record your own thoughts that come to you as you reflect on the psalm. Skip any psalm or part of it that has no meaning for you. Don't get hung up on a sentence or word you don't understand. Just skip and look for the next sentence that has a message for you. The one thing common to all psalms is that they are talking to God. Many claim to have gotten a response in dialogue.

My own faith leaves many questions unanswered. However, it gives me the one thing I most need: the assurance that life is not a vanity of vanities, that there is more to life than the meaningless absurdity voiced by Macbeth:

> Life's but a walking shadow, a poor player
> That struts and frets this hour upon the stage
> And then is heard no more. It is a tale
> Told by an idiot, full of sound and fury,
> Signifying nothing.
> (*Macbeth*, V, v, 17)

I am impressed by the atheistic assault on God and our connection with Him, but not convinced. I still believe in God as Creator and pray to God daily, when retiring for the night and upon awakening in the morning.

For me, the most moving witness to faith is an inscription found in the German city of Cologne, scribbled on the wall of a dark cellar in which some Jews had been hiding out during the war:

> I believe in the sun when it is not shining.
> I believe in love even when feeling it not.
> I believe in God even when He is silent.

The problem for many is that prayers go unanswered. For others, the problem is simply non-belief in God. A large majority of people say they believe in God but doubt that God cares and listens to each human being. With such doubts, prayer becomes a monologue or talking to a wall.

We Jews are not Holocaust deniers but many of us are God

deniers. "Where was God when we most needed Him?" This question is on the lips of those whose prayers have not been answered. Does God pay attention to our cry for help? A number of psalmists challenge God: "Where are You when I need You?" Psalm 88 is bitter: "Will You work wonders for me when I am dead?" (Ps. 88.11)

Speaking personally, when I say the Sh'ma 'Yisrael—"Hear, O Israel," something within me cries out: "Hear, O God—Do You hear my prayer? Are You listening to me?"

Then, I stop to think, isn't it colossal *chutzpah* on my part to ask the Supreme Being, while minding the Universe, to bother with me and my needs, me, a speck of dust in this immeasurable universe? One of our daily prayers stresses man's insignificance: "What are we? What is our life.? Our power? Our strength? Are not all the men of might as nothing before You, their works empty and their lives a mere breath before You?"

Why should God be concerned with each of us individually? Can we expect the Supreme power and intelligence of the universe to share our anguish over a troubled child? Or, worry with us about our stock-portfolio? Or, is it imaginable that God will intervene to relieve my rheumatism and help me sleep?

My rationality argues that the notion of God hearing and answering prayer may be wishful thinking, absurd and utterly improbable.

Am I so important that God wants to hear from me? Is He pleased when I pray?

The answer is anybody's guess. Then, why go on praying?

My reason for continuing the practice is that no one knows or ever shall know the impact of our prayers upon God. I only know my side, what I do in prayer. God's side is unknowable. No one knows what our prayer means to God.

Despite all these doubts, if, any of my children were gravely ill, I would pray for my child's recovery anyhow, on the chance that God listens and might respond in totally unpredictable ways. As Hamlet pointed out to Horatio, "There are more things in heaven and on earth than are dreamt of in your philosophy." (*Hamlet* I, v, 166)

It was said in wartime, "There are no atheists in the foxholes."

No doubt, even skeptics will pray in a crisis. The novelist Mary Austin said, "You'd be surprised how much I learned about prayer from playing poker."

Is prayer a crutch? Yes, and we need it!

The foremost object of prayer is not begging but connecting with God. The content of the prayer makes little difference; it doesn't matter if the prayer is in English or Hebrew. What counts is that in praying I am reaching out on a spiritual wavelength to connect with God.

The author of Psalm 73 was shaken by the realization that the law of reward and punishment doesn't work as expected. Until one day, while praying in the sanctuary, he had a powerful sense of God's presence, of being connected with the Eternal One. Nothing else mattered. So he exclaimed, "As for me, being near God is my good."

Good in what way? Feeling connected with God, he felt no longer like a speck of dust. He gained a higher importance. He was part of the Eternal God.

Prayer, then, is outreach to God. But, what if you don't feel this connection with God? Think of it this way: If you call a friend and no one picks up the phone or you get a busy signal, what do you do? You don't give up. You don't say, "I'll never call him again." You try again and again until your call goes through. So it is with prayer. One or several attempts to connect with God may not be enough. If you pray often enough, you may finally get the connection. The value of persistent prayer is not that God will hear us, but that we will finally hear Him.

Conclusion

The Chinese pictograph for the word "crisis" has two parts, which signify "danger" and "opportunity." Every crisis may shake us up, emotionally and physically. It will cause us pain and loss. It will also change our outlook on life. But with that change may come some gains, opening of the eyes, new vision, a new way of looking at ourselves, at our relationships, and at our goals in life. A crisis will surely make us sit up and listen to truths we may have long ignored. Crises lead to discoveries. They are learning experiences, albeit, at a high price.

Illness cuts us down to size. It drives home the truth of our limitations, our dependence, and the uncertainty of human existence. But we may also gain from illness a measure of humility and gratitude for every day of good health. Our pain may make us more understanding and compassionate of others.

Failure and defeat are always bitter pills to swallow, but in some respect they are good medicine for our mentality. A failure should prompt us to reassess our lives, our goals, our way with people. Defeat should tell us that we can't do everything, a realization which may turn our life around and move us into a better direction.

Painful as rejection may be, it can also be the springboard to great achievement if, trying to prove our worth, we bring out the best there is in us.

Marriage is the greatest character test. Two persons with two different minds are bound to clash. Living together inevitably entails a contest of wills. When husband and wife are in dispute, and no argument can persuade the other, they must find a compromise. But failing to find it, one or the other spouse must have enough love in his or her heart to make a sacrifice and yield to the wish of the spouse for the sake of the marriage.

We shall never know the meaning of life. It is the secret of the Creator. Since none of us came into this world by his own will, we shall keep wondering if our life is a gift, a mission for some purpose, or a phenomenon of meaningless chance. Not even people of faith can prove that life has meaning. But having faith, they need no such proof.

It is odd that all want to live longer but not get older. With life expectancy twice, even three times what it used to be, we need to come to terms with old age. The balance sheet of every stage in life will show gains and losses. The physical decline of old age may be compensated by mental growth, greater understanding, and wisdom. But this can only happen to those who throughout their earlier years set aside time to learn, think, reflect, and cultivate a spiritual life.

Life is wrapped up in two mysteries: its origin and what seems to be its ending. Death may be clinically defined as the cessation of physical functions and disintegration. But is death a total ending? an ultimate extinction? We cannot answer with certainty. Fears inspired by death are best relieved by a sense of connection with all there is. The belief that we are part of a greater whole is the heart of religious faith.

Bibliography and Notes

The following works are quoted in the text:

A Rabbinic Anthology by C.G. Montefiore and H. M. J. Loewe, Macmillan & Co., London, 1938

A Maimonides Reader by Isadore Twersky, Library of Jewish Studies, 1972

Gift from the Sea by Ann Morrow Lindbergh, Pantheon Books, 1955

Guide of the Perplexed by Moses Maimonides, University of California Libraries, 1885

Introduction to the Code of Maimonides (Mishneh Torah) by Isadore Twersky, Yale Judaica Series, 1982

Nichomean Ethics by Aristotle

The Secret Life of Bees by Sue Monk Kidd, Penguin Books, 2002

The Sphere and Duties of Woman: A Course of Lectures, Lecture IV, p. 99), John Murphy, Baltimore, 1948

Tuesdays with Morrie by Mitch Albom, Doubleday, 1997

Whatever Became of Sin by Karl Menninger, Hawthorn, 1974

"Happiness Rx: What Science Says" interview with Sonja Lyubomirsky, *Reform Judaism Magazine*, Winter 2011

In addition, many passages are from the *Bible*, the *Midrash* (Bereshit Rabbah and Exodus Rabbah) and the *Talmud* (Berakot, Eruvin, Kiddushin, and Pirke Avot).

About the Author

Born in Vienna, Austria, Rabbi Joshua O. Haberman was a student at the Rabbinical Seminary and the University of Vienna when the Nazi invasion of 1938 forced him to flee his native country. He continued his studies at the Hebrew Union College and the University of Cincinnati, was ordained as rabbi, and earned a doctorate in modern Jewish theology.

Prior to his election as Senior Rabbi at the Washington Hebrew Congregation in 1969, he served as Interim Rabbi in Mobile, Alabama, Assistant Rabbi at Temple Beth Zion of Buffalo, and Rabbi of Har Sinai Temple in Trenton.

He has taught as an adjunct professor in all Washington area universities, preached at the White House, published four books, and written scholarly papers, including articles in the Encyclopedia Judaica. He is the founding chairman of the Foundation for Jewish Studies, the largest provider of Jewish adult study programs in the Washington area, and Rabbi Emeritus of Washington Hebrew Congregation.

He lives in Rockville, Maryland, and keeps a second home in Jerusalem to be near his large family in Israel.